# *beautiful*
# HOPE

## FINDING HOPE EVERY DAY IN A BROKEN WORLD

BEACON PUBLISHING

North Palm Beach, Florida

ISBN: 978-1-929266-53-1 (hardcover)
ISBN: 978-1-929266-54-8 (softcover)
ISBN: 978-1-929266-95-1 (e-book)

Design by Jenny Miller
Interior by Ashley Wirfel

Unless otherwise noted, Scripture passages have been taken from
the *Revised Standard Version, Catholic Edition*. Copyright 1946, 1952, 1971 by the Division
of Christian Education of the National Council of Churches
of Christ in the USA. Used by permission. All rights reserved.

Quotes are taken from the English translation of the *Catechism of the Catholic Church* for
the United States of America (indicated as *CCC*), 2nd ed. Copyright 1997 by United States
Catholic Conference—Libreria Editrice Vaticana.

Introduction excerpted from 2016 papal audiences given by Pope Francis in the Paul
VI Audience Hall on Wednesday, December 7; Wednesday, December 14; and Wednesday,
December 21; found on the Holy See website, w2.vatican.va.

Library of Congress Cataloging-in-Publication Data
Names: Beacon Publishing.
Title: Beautiful hope : finding hope every day in a broken world.
Description: North Palm Beach, Florida : Beacon Publishing, Inc., 2017.
Identifiers: LCCN 2017029598 | ISBN 9781929266531 (hard cover :
alk. paper) | ISBN 9781929266548 (soft cover : alk. paper) | ISBN
9781929266951 (e-book : alk. paper)
Subjects: LCSH: Hope—Religious aspects—Christianity—Meditations.
| Hope—Religious aspects—Christianity—Anecdotes.
Classification: LCC BV4638 .B43 2017 | DDC
234/.25—dc23

Dynamic Catholic® and Be Bold. Be Catholic.® and
The Best Version of Yourself® are registered trademarks of
The Dynamic Catholic Institute.

For more information on bulk copies of this title or other books and CDs
available through the Dynamic Catholic Book Program,
please visit www.DynamicCatholic.com or call 859-980-7900.

The Dynamic Catholic Institute
5081 Olympic Blvd • Erlanger • Kentucky • 41018
Phone: 1–859–980–7900
Email: info@DynamicCatholic.com

Second printing, December 2017

Printed in the United States of America

# TABLE OF CONTENTS

# PRELUDE

*MATTHEW KELLY*

*"Man can live forty days without food, about three days*
*without water, about eight minutes without air,*
*but only one second without hope."*
*— Unknown*

It was Paul's time. He could see it in the doctor's eyes. After ninety-two years of life, Paul was ready to go back to God. His last request was to spend a private moment with each special person gathered around his bed.

Three children, five grandchildren, a coworker, and two lifelong friends shared the final hours of Paul's life. Words of love, appreciation, and forgiveness. Tears of sorrow. Tears of laughter. Each person left the room feeling lighter than they had felt in years. Peace came with each encounter. A peace that only comes from spending time with a life well lived.

Outside, in the waiting area, nervous and a bit scared, Connor waited for his turn. Connor was Paul's grandson. When Connor was ten, his dad left him, his mother, and his two younger brothers. Connor's mom, Paul's daughter,

2 • BEAUTIFUL HOPE

wanted her three sons to have a strong male role model, so she moved the family into her father's house. A recent widower, Paul was thankful for the company.

In the early years, Paul had taught Connor everything he knew: how to fish, how to live as a man of integrity, and how to pray. In the later years the roles had changed. As Paul's body began to fail him, Connor had taken his grandfather to Mass on Sunday; he had helped him get dressed in the morning and ready for bed at night; and he had stayed up late with him listening to old Frank Sinatra records when Paul had been in too much pain to sleep. The two men loved each other at a level words could not express.

But Connor wasn't yet ready to say good-bye. Paul was his rock, his role model, and his best friend. Connor wondered how he would navigate life without him. Connor was the last one to visit his grandfather. He walked in and sat down next to Paul, who had his eyes closed. When he opened his eyes, Paul smiled at his grandson. Immediately Connor began to weep. "I don't want to lose you!" he shouted and buried his head in his grandfather's chest.

Paul took a deep breath and savored the moment. He remembered the day Connor had been born, how he had fit in the palm of his hand. Paul thanked God for sending him such a friend so late in life. Paul lifted his grandson's chin so they could look each other in the eye. "Son, we'll always be together, you know that. Just pray for me on this side of heaven and know I'll be praying for you on the other. Then one day we'll meet again." He wiped the tears from his grandson's eyes; they shared a smile and hugged one last time.

That's beautiful hope.

For some time Brian had been feeling restless, like something was missing. He couldn't figure out why. He had a good job. He provided well for his wife and two kids. He had a nice marriage. Sure, the passion wasn't really there anymore, but that happens with age. For the most part, his kids were well behaved. He loved them, and they knew it. On most Sundays the family went to Mass together. Life was good. He was a good guy. So what was wrong? Why couldn't he just be happy?

On his way to work each day, Brian passed St. Patrick's, his parish church. Recently something had always seemed to be tugging at him to go inside. For weeks he had ignored it and told himself it would pass. But it hadn't. The nudging had continued.

Finally, Brian went into the church, not because he thought it would help, but to prove a point. He thought that if he just went in and sat there for ten minutes, nothing would happen, and he could move on with his life. But instead, the stillness swallowed Brian whole. He instantly liked how quiet it was. Everything in his life was so loud; the silence was actually comforting . . . peaceful.

Brian began to daydream about heaven. He wondered what it would be like to stand before God. He wondered how God would feel about the halfhearted way he was living his life. He wondered if God would think he was a good husband and father. And at that thought a deep feeling of dissatisfaction nearly overwhelmed Brian.

Suddenly life felt incredibly short. Work problems, his to-do list at home, and whether or not the Indianapolis Colts would win on Sunday took a backseat in his mind. Brian began to wonder when he had last looked into the eyes of his wife and really listened to what she had to say. He thought of the car sitting in his garage and the promise he had made to his son that they would fix it up together. He thought of his daughter and how they had done nothing but argue for months. He thought about the last time he had prayed to God . . . really, truly prayed.

Brian went back to his parish church the next day. And the day after. And the day after that. He formed a new habit of just sitting in silence. And talking to God. He thought about his life. He thought about heaven. Then he started making a plan with God. He made a plan to change his life.

That's beautiful hope.

---

Not long ago I was at a conference here in Cincinnati, and a woman stopped me. "I'm sorry to bother you," she said, "but I just want to thank you."

I stopped walking, and we shook hands. She began to tell me the story of her husband. Of how he had come to one of my Living Every Day with Passion and Purpose events and how God had moved his heart in a powerful way. She told me how the genius of Catholicism had changed his life and how he had become the husband and father she had always dreamed he could be.

She told me about the day of his accident. About what it was like to get a phone call from a stranger saying that your husband had just died. She talked of the heart-wrenching experience of telling their children that their father was never coming home. She spoke of the pain of going to sleep alone that first night.

Then she shared about the day before the funeral and an idea she'd had. In the last year of her husband's life he had tried to share the love of God with as many people as he could. She laughed as she recalled her children's embarrassment as their dad shamelessly handed out Catholic books and CDs to anyone and everyone.

She told me that the day before the funeral, she had called our team at Dynamic Catholic in desperation. She said she had begged one of our Mission Team members to rush-order two of her husband's favorite audio CDs. To honor him, she had wanted to give the CDs as a gift to everyone who attended his funeral.

Before she left she thanked me again. She thanked me for inspiring her husband and helping God change her family's life for the better. And she asked me to pass a thank-you along to my team for going above and beyond when she had needed it most.

I was deeply moved as I watched her leave. I may never see her again, but if I do, I will be the one who will be thanking her. I will thank her for two reasons.

First, her story reminded me that it's never too late for a new beginning. Her husband had discovered that. It's never too late to start over again. It's never too late to choose to become the-best-version-of-yourself. She reminded me that God wants us to be people of possibility, and people of possibility never give up.

The second reason is that she reminded me why we started Dynamic Catholic in the first place. It's because we believe our future can be bigger than our past.

If you ever come to visit our team, you will find our mission statement written in large, bold letters when you walk through the front doors of the office. It reads: *The mission of Dynamic Catholic is to re-energize the Catholic Church in America by developing world-class resources that inspire people to rediscover the genius of Catholicism.*

Our mission statement creates more than just an explanation of what we aim to accomplish. It's a declaration of what's possible. It's a mission of hope.

For this book, we've enlisted the help of some incredible people to capture the power of hope. Each author was asked to write on any or all of the following topics: What gives you hope? What sustains your hope? Where does your hope for the Catholic Church come from? What are your hopes for the Catholic Church and humanity? How do you bring hope to others?

Some of the authors in this book are professional authors and speakers, but many are not. Many have never published anything ever before. They are everyday American Catholics doing their best to live the gospel. The reason for this is simple: God's hope can be experienced and spread at any age, in any state of life, anytime, anywhere. All it takes is an open heart and a willing spirit.

When I first had the idea for this book, I asked members of the team at Dynamic Catholic to tell me about the one person in their life who brought them the most hope. Nearly every single one of them shared with me the person in their life who had suffered the most. Should it be any surprise that the light shines brightest in the darkest night?

These are trying times for people of faith. The Church has been through a lot these last twenty years. As I travel around the country, it seems that we are all less hopeful than we were twenty years ago. We are less hopeful when we think about the future for our families and loved ones. And we are less hopeful for the future of the Church.

If we are to become the people and the Church God dreams of us becoming, this must change. We need hope. After all, hope is a good thing, maybe the best of things. Hope is the one thing you can't buy, but that will be given to you freely if you ask. Hope is the one thing people cannot live without.

What we read today walks and talks with us tomorrow. We truly do become what we read. I hope this book walks and talks with you so much that God fills your whole mind, your whole body, and your whole soul with hope. I hope you feel proud to be Catholic. We are a people of hope. And our future is even brighter than our past.

How will you bring hope to others today?

---

Matthew Kelly is the *New York Times* bestselling author of *The Rhythm of Life* and twenty other books, including *Rediscover Jesus*.

# INTRODUCTION: NEVER LOSE HOPE

*POPE FRANCIS*

Hope never disappoints. Optimism disappoints, but hope does not! We have such need, in these times which appear dark. We need hope! We feel disoriented and even rather discouraged, because we are powerless, and it seems this darkness will never end.

We must not let hope abandon us, because God, with his love, walks with us. "I hope, because God is beside me": we can all say this. Each one of us can say: "I hope, I have hope, because God walks with me." He walks and he holds my hand. God does not leave us to ourselves. The Lord Jesus has conquered evil and has opened the path of life for us . . .

Let us listen to the words of Sacred Scripture, beginning with the prophet Isaiah . . . the great messenger of hope.

In the second part of his book, Isaiah addresses the people with his message of comfort: "Comfort, comfort my people, says your God. Speak tenderly to Jerusalem, and cry to her that her warfare is ended, that her iniquity is pardoned. . . . A voice cries: 'In the wilderness prepare the way of the Lord, make straight in the desert a highway for our God. Every valley shall be lifted up, and every mountain and hill be made low; the uneven ground shall become level, and the rough places a plain. And the glory of the Lord shall be revealed, and all flesh shall see it together, for the mouth of the Lord has spoken'" (Isaiah 40:1-2, 3-5). . . .

The Exile was a fraught moment in the history of Israel, when the people had lost everything. The people had lost their homeland, freedom, dignity, and even trust in God. They felt abandoned and hopeless. Instead, however, there is the prophet's appeal which reopens the heart to faith. The desert is a place in which it is difficult to live, but precisely there, one can now walk in order to return not only to the homeland, but return to God, and return to hoping and smiling. When we are in darkness, in difficulty, we do not smile, and it is precisely hope which teaches us to smile in order to find the path that leads to God. One of the first things that happens to people who distance themselves from God is that they are people who do not smile. Perhaps they can break into a loud laugh, one after another, a joke, a chuckle . . . but their smile is missing! Only hope brings a smile: it is the hopeful smile in the expectation of finding God.

Life is often a desert, it is difficult to walk in life, but if we trust in God, it can become beautiful and wide as a highway. Just never lose hope, just continue to believe, always, in spite of everything. . . . Each one knows what desert he or she is walking in—it will become a garden in bloom. Hope does not disappoint!

The prophet Isaiah once again helps us to open ourselves to the hope of welcoming the Good News of the coming of salvation.

———————

Isaiah chapter 52 begins with the invitation addressed to Jerusalem to awake, shake off the dust and chains, and put on the most beautiful clothes, because the Lord has come to free his people (verses 1–3). And he adds: "[M]y people shall know my name; therefore in that day they shall know that it is I who speak; here am I" (verse 6). It is to this "here am I" said by the Lord, which sums up his firm will for salvation and closeness to us, that Jerusalem responds with a song of joy, according to the prophet's invitation . . .

These are the words of faith in a Lord whose power bends down to humanity, stoops down, to offer mercy and to free man and woman from all that disfigures in them the beautiful image of God, for when we are in sin, God's image is disfigured. The fulfillment of so much love will be the very Kingdom instituted by Jesus, that Kingdom of forgiveness and peace which we celebrate at Christmas, and which is definitively achieved at Easter . . .

These are, brothers and sisters, the reasons for our hope. When everything seems finished, when, faced with many negative realities, and faith becomes demanding, and there comes the temptation which says that nothing makes sense anymore, behold instead the beautiful news . . . God is coming to fulfill something new, to establish a kingdom of peace . . . Evil will not triumph forever; there is an end to suffering. Despair is defeated because God is among us.

And we too are urged to awake a little, like Jerusalem, according to the invitation of the prophet; we are called to become men and women of hope, cooperating in the coming of this Kingdom made of light and destined for all, men and women of hope . . . God destroys such walls with forgiveness! And for this reason we must pray, that each day God may give us hope and give it to everyone: that hope which arises when we see God in the crib in Bethlehem. The message of the Good News entrusted to us is urgent . . .

---

It was also Isaiah who foretold the birth of the Messiah in several passages: "Behold, a young woman shall conceive and bear a son, and shall call his name Immanuel" (Isaiah 7:14); and also: "there shall come forth a shoot from the stump of Jesse, and a branch shall grow out of his roots" (Isaiah 11:1). In these passages, the meaning of Christmas shines through: God fulfills the promise by becoming man; not abandoning his people, he draws near to the point of stripping himself of his divinity. In this way God shows his fidelity and inaugurates a new Kingdom, which gives a new hope to mankind. And what is this hope? Eternal life.

When we speak of hope, often it refers to what is not in man's power to realize, which is invisible. In fact, what we hope for goes beyond our strength and our perception. But the Birth of Christ, inaugurating redemption, speaks to us of a different hope, a dependable, visible, and understandable hope, because it is founded in God. He comes into the world and gives us the strength to walk with him: God walks with us in Jesus, and walking with him toward the fullness of life gives us the strength to dwell in the present in a new way, albeit arduous. Thus for a Christian, to hope means the certainty of being on a journey with Christ toward the Father who awaits us. Hope is never still; hope is always journeying, and it makes us journey. This hope, which the Child of Bethlehem gives us, offers a destination, a sure, ongoing goal, salvation of mankind, blessedness to those who trust in a merciful God. Saint Paul summarizes all this with the expression: "in this hope we were saved" (Romans 8:24). In other words, walking in this world, with hope, we are saved. Here we can ask ourselves the question, each one of us: Am I walking with hope, or is my interior life static, closed? Is my heart a locked drawer or a drawer open to the hope which enables me to walk—not alone—with Jesus? . . .

Those who trust in their own certainties, especially material, do not await God's salvation. Let us keep this in mind: our own assurance will not save us; the only certainty that will save us is that of hope in God. It will save us because it is strong and enables us to journey in life with joy, with the will to do good, with the will to attain eternal happiness . . .

Christian hope is expressed in praise and gratitude to God, who has initiated his Kingdom of love, justice, and peace. . . . It will truly be a celebration if we welcome Jesus, the seed of hope that God sets down in the furrows of our individual and community history. Every "yes" to Jesus who comes, is a bud of hope. Let us trust in this bud of hope, in this "yes": "Yes, Jesus, you can save me, you can save me."

# PART ONE

# CHOOSING HOPE

*"The Lord is my portion," says my soul,*
*"therefore I will hope in him."*

*—LAMENTATIONS 3:24*

# A POWERFUL FORCE

## FR. MIKE SCHMITZ

*"To have Christian hope means to know about evil and
yet to go to meet the future with confidence."*
— *Pope Benedict XVI*

How does one live with hope? This world seems so lost at times. Even more personally, our lives seem so painful and senseless at times. It all just seems so pointless.

If you have ever asked this question, that is a very good sign. It is a sign that you have a certain degree of hope, because you have taken action in asking for an answer. And hope is almost always going to be connected to action.

Years ago, I read Laura Hillenbrand's phenomenal book *Unbroken*. It is the story of the life of a man named Louis Zamperini. Louie grew up in California in the early part of the twentieth century. He was relatively "wild" as a child, and his older brother convinced their high-school principal to give Louie a chance to stay out of trouble by letting him join the school track team. At first Louis was absolutely no good at running, but under the constant coaching of his older brother, he soon became the fastest miler in California state history. He even competed in the 1936 Olympic Games in Berlin. After he returned from Berlin, war broke out across Europe and the Pacific. Louis joined the Air Force and soon found himself flying a B-24 bomber in the South Pacific.

On one of these runs, the bomber crashed into the ocean and only three men survived: Louis and two of his crewmates. They spent the next forty-seven days drifting under the blazing hot sun of the South Pacific Ocean, constantly hungry, perpetually thirsty, and often threatened and attacked by sharks. With their life raft constantly leaking, they had to continually do their best to patch and keep it inflated. The sharks were so bold that, multiple times, they launched themselves up onto the raft in an attempt to snag one of the three men.

Desperate, nearly mad, and hopeless, one of the men, Francis McNamara, ultimately succumbed to despair and died aboard the raft. Louis and the other survivor, Russell Allen Phillips, lived to finally make it to land. At one point, Laura Hillenbrand noted,

> Given the dismal record of raft-bound men, Mac's despair was reasonable. What is remarkable is that the two men who shared Mac's plight didn't share his hopelessness. Though all three faced the same hardship, their differing perceptions of it appeared to be shaping their fates.

Hope is powerful. Hopelessness is also powerful.

But these two things are not powerful in and of themselves. What I mean to say is, hope is not merely optimism or wishful thinking. Often people I work with who share their desire to live in hope seem to reveal that what they really long for is optimism. While optimism can be a nice thing for most people on most days, it is virtually useless when needed the most.

Another former military man who is familiar with long-suffering and brutality is Admiral Jim Stockdale. Admiral Stockdale was captured during the Vietnam War and kept in a POW camp for eight horrendous years. Since he was the highest-ranking American in the Viet Cong camp, he was often tortured more and submitted to more brutal treatment than the other soldiers in order to break him. Nonetheless, all of the men in the POW camp were exposed to terrible treatment and torture. When Admiral Stockade returned to the United States, years later he was asked about the difference between the men who lived through the ordeal and those who succumbed to the harsh treatment and ended up being crushed by it. In his book, *Good to Great*, author Jim Collins asked him about those who were the first to be defeated by their situation. Admiral Stockdale replied:

> Oh, that's easy, the optimists. Oh, they were the ones who said, "We're going to be out by Christmas." And Christmas would come, and Christmas would go. Then they'd say, "We're going to be out by Easter." And Easter would come, and Easter would go. And then Thanksgiving, and then it would be Christmas again. And they died of a broken heart.

Stockdale, and the others who survived, however, had a different attitude. They fought to live. Their perspective was completely different than those who merely wished for rescue or were optimistic about freedom. They acted. And they acted based on one clear and fundamental belief: Life has meaning. Stockdale continued:

> I never lost faith in the end of the story, I never doubted not only that I would get out, but also that I would prevail in the end and turn the experience into the defining event of my life, which, in retrospect, I would not trade.

The Admiral recognized that, while the moment in which he was living did not seem to make any sense (constant torture and solitary confinement), he was part of a greater story. Realizing this, he had the power to be an "actor" in his own story. While he was not in control of everything that happened to him, Stockdale could control some things. He was willing to act when and how he had the power to act.

Living like this did not mean burying his head in the sand and merely "wishing" things would change. It meant facing reality and working toward that change. Again in his own words,

> You must never confuse faith that you will prevail in the end— which you can never afford to lose—with the discipline to confront the most brutal facts of your current reality, whatever they might be.

Those with hope are willing to act. Those without hope are content to wish.

If you desire to be a person of hope, a person who has the will that what is good might be reality, you must be a person of two things: meaning and action.

We live in a hopeless age. Don't get me wrong—there is an awful lot of optimism, but very little hope. The source of this hopelessness is a profound lack of meaning in most people's lives. Many of us live our lives looking forward to "the next thing." We say things like, "It might be rough now, but once I get that promotion, then I'll be fine." Or, "I know that I'm lonely now, but once I find someone, then I'll be fine." Or, "I know that my spouse and I are discontented now, but once we have kids, then we will be fine." Or the thousand other things we look forward to that will help us to be "fine." There is nothing wrong with looking forward to something, but sooner or later we discover that it just doesn't deliver. We go on to the next thing and are no better off. We miss the meaning of the moments of our lives because we have forgotten that all of life is meaningful.

This is why being a Christian—a real follower of Jesus Christ—is a game changer. All of us experience the pain that the world throws at us. All of us experience discouragement and even utter destruction (i.e., we are all going to die someday). Like Admiral Stockdale and Louis Zamperini, all of us will be confronted with situations where we cannot escape and where wishing isn't enough. As Christians, we know that God has made this world good. We know that evil and suffering and death are not a part of his plan for our lives, but that he is with us in the midst of even the worst and most destructive storms. We know he can work out for the good everything that comes against his children. We have this hope, this confidence, that our lives have meaning.

And if our lives have meaning, then all our choices have meaning too. Many people are paralyzed by their situations or their fears. Too many of us look at the challenges of the moment and choose to "wish" rather than to hope. But wishing is hopelessness in disguise. It leads nowhere. Hope leads us to action. Hillenbrand described the difference between the men in the raft:

> Louie's and Phil's hope displaced their fear and inspired them to work toward their survival, and each success renewed their physical and emotional vigor. Mac's resignation seemed to paralyze him, and the less he participated in their efforts to survive, the more he slipped.

How does a person grow in hope? By reconnecting with God's story. By being reminded that we believe that there is more to this life than just this life. By being committed to the truth that God is in all things and all moments and that our decisions matter. And then . . . then simply beginning to make choices. Decide. Act on those decisions. You cannot do everything, but you can do something. Do what you can, and you will find that hope has become a powerful force in your life.

---

**FOCUS:** We have this hope, this confidence, that our lives have meaning. And if our lives have meaning, then all our choices have meaning too.

**REFLECT:** What gives your life meaning?

*Fr. Mike Schmitz is the chaplain for Newman Catholic Campus Ministry at the University of Minnesota Duluth.*

# THE TRIUMPH OF HOPE

## SR. MIRIAM JAMES HEIDLAND, SOLT

*"All shall be well, and all shall be well,*
*and all manner of thing shall be well in the end."*
— Jesus' words to Julian of Norwich

It is every traveler's biggest irritation—a connecting flight at the other end of the airport when your arriving plane has landed an hour late. A mad rush ensues, and it was in this very situation that I found myself one evening at one of the biggest airports in the world. As I packed myself into the airport tram en route to the connecting terminal, I mentally willed the tram to go faster, while my anxiety rose and a plan B swirled in my head to employ in the probable event that I missed this flight.

The tram doors whooshed open and I pushed my way out of the crowd and onto the escalator only to hear the "last call" announcement for my flight blaring through the speakers overhead. Then and there I made the decision to give new meaning to the term "flying nun," and I took off sprinting. Veil flying, carry-on bag hitting me in the legs, I bolted down the terminal hallway to the amusement of passers-by, in the vain hope that I would make it to the gate before the imposing door closed on the flight, banishing me to a night spent in uncomfortable airport chairs.

Finally approaching the sought-after gate, I could barely get the words out of my mouth as I breathlessly stumbled up to the counter. The flummoxed gate agent heard something like, "Did . . . I . . . (cough, cough) . . . make . . . it?"

Staring at the disheveled nun in front of her, she replied, "You barely made it. Please hurry and take your seat."

I gratefully scooped up my bag and rubbed my sore knee as I quickly made my way down the ramp, all the while pondering with astonishment the fact that my hope—my "wish"—had come true. I suddenly also realized that much of my adult understanding of hope had been just that: wishful thinking.

The dictionary defines *hope* as "the feeling that what is wanted can be had or that events will turn out for the best."[1] It also defines *wish* as "to want; desire; long for."[2] While these definitions are technically true, they fall short of the meaning of the hope that God infuses within us as a theological virtue. For people of faith, the truest meaning of hope is not ultimately a feeling or a longing toward a vague (or even a specific) temporal good, but rather a gift from God that orders us toward eternal goodness, truth, and beauty—a gift that orders us toward eternal union with himself.

The difference in how hope is defined may sound like a technicality, but it reveals something profound. For a long time I thought that hope in God was the same thing as hoping I got a good grade on an exam—or hoping my flight would actually be on time. It was something I wanted to happen, but something that may just as well not happen. I hoped God would hear my prayer; I hoped he would bring joy out of my suffering; I hoped he would heal a world broken by sin and death. But would he?

All of us have sorrowful mysteries in our lives. We all have those parts of our hearts and lives that are rarely spoken of, preferably forgotten, and hidden in darkness. We all have family members who are struggling. We all see the suffering of humanity across the world, and I think we all wonder at times, "Why would a good God allow these things to happen?" It's often in these moments, in the acute sorrow and the chronic suffering, that hope can die in our hearts.

Over the years I have needed to have many words rehabilitated in my heart and mind. My life was profoundly transformed when both mercy and forgiveness were restored and more properly understood. This very same thing is happening now in my life as God rehabilitates the word hope and its meaning in the depths of my heart. Hope is not merely a wish that something good might happen—it is the firm confidence and desire that the promises of God will be fulfilled. It is the expectation that "he who began a good work among you will bring it to completion" (Philippians 1:6).

If you have ever seen a "fixer-upper" TV show where a person buys a house in need of repair, you've probably seen an episode in which the structural damage of the house is so deep that the construction crew has to dig down to the very foundation and start over. They have to remove the concrete, reinforce the beams, pour new concrete, and level the house. It is a massive and expensive undertaking, but many times it is the only option for salvaging and restoring a home that will stand strong for years into the future.

In many ways, I feel as though this is what God has been doing in my life for a long time. My foundation had some major cracks in it right from the start. My "house" carried the structural damage of being conceived out of wedlock and then given up for adoption, the emotional and spiritual scars of sexual abuse as a child, a battle with alcoholism, chronic low-grade depression, and an overwhelming loss of hope. My way of dealing with this damage was to "paint the exterior," deny the depth of the problems, or just try to fix them myself. All of these coping mechanisms failed, and I felt very alone, very unloved, and very hopeless.

The interesting paradox of our humanity is that it is often not until we come to the end of our own resources that we finally begin to surrender to God. In his kindness, God began to firmly but gently excavate the depths of my foundation, and he continues to do so to this very day. He removes the weakened beams of self-reliance and the hard concrete of shame. He strengthens my frame with his truth and pours his love into my gaping heart. He levels me with his beauty and turns my gaze toward him in hope as the Master Builder, the Lover of my soul.

It is long and exacting work. Sometimes it happens quickly and sometimes slowly, but the more I surrender all of myself to him, the more hope builds in my heart. God desires our good. Suffering does not have the last say. It is not the end of the story. God brings beauty out of sorrow and resurrection from the cross. We are not forgotten. This is not wishful thinking. He loves us.

God promises that he will be with us always, that he will never leave us, and that one day, if we choose him, we shall see him as he is. On that day, we shall become one with the One who loves us. This truth gives vibrancy to all we long for in life, and it gives color to our deep hope for eternal life with him.

---

**FOCUS:** Hope is not merely a wish that something good might happen—it is the firm confidence and desire that the promises of God will be fulfilled.

**REFLECT:** Where are the cracks in your foundation, and how can the Master Builder repair them?

*Sr. Miriam James is a member of the Society of Our Lady of the Most Holy Trinity (SOLT). She speaks internationally on the topics of authentic love, healing, and conversion and is the author of the book* Loved as I Am.

# EXPECT THE IMPOSSIBLE

## FR. JACQUES PHILIPPE

*"One obtains from God all that one hopes from him!"*
— *St. John of the Cross*

"The faith that I love the best, says God, is hope." The French poet Charles Péguy put these words on God's lips at the beginning of his book *The Portal of the Mystery of Hope*. It is one of the most beautiful books ever written about hope.

Hope is, so to speak, the most Christian virtue of all. The main characteristic of our lives as Christians should be the fact that we always look at things with hope: at life, the future, ourselves, other people, and so on.

It is not always easy. Very often the future worries us, other people disappoint us, and we doubt ourselves. Humanly speaking, there are plenty of reasons for losing hope, and sometimes they may seem overpowering. However, in spite of everything, hope should always stand firm in our hearts and have the last word, to the point where we "hope against hope," as St. Paul says of Abraham (see Romans 4:18). Because if we lose hope, we lose everything.

Hope plays a key role in the spiritual life. It is based on faith—faith in God's fidelity to his promises, and faith in Christ's victory—and it enables charity to flourish. Faith and hope are like the wings of love; they give love the power to launch out ever further, to take flight unceasingly, without getting exhausted or discouraged. When hope dwindles, love also dies down; the heart is invaded by uneasiness and worry, which stifle charity. Hope keeps the heart free to love, and to give itself.

Hope is important because it goes hand in hand with desire. Desire is the only infinite thing man possesses, says St. Catherine of Siena.[3] Human beings are beings of desires: Their desires are the measure of their vitality. Christian life does not aim to extinguish or reject desires, but to purify desire and orientate it toward the only good that can really fulfill it: the Supreme Good, which is God.

We need to ask ourselves: "What is my deepest desire? What is the one aspiration that unifies my whole life?" Growing in hope means opening ourselves to the work of the Holy Spirit so we can learn progressively to desire what God desires for us, to hope for what God hopes for with regard to us, which is always greater than we can imagine. The theological virtue of hope orientates our desire toward God, nurtures it, stirs it up when necessary, and protects it against any temptation to discouragement.

Hope makes possible something that is, humanly speaking, impossible. It makes us confidently expect everything from God, and obtain from him the grace and help necessary to respond to our vocation.

St. Thérèse of Lisieux entered Carmel at the age of fifteen, with a burning desire for holiness. She wanted to become a great saint, to love Jesus as much as he can possibly be loved, and to be useful to the Church. But her great desires contrasted with the hard test of reality. She had experience of her own limitations and flaws, as she herself explained: "I have always noticed that when I compared myself with the saints, there is between them and me the same difference that exists between a mountain whose summit is lost in the clouds and the obscure grain of sand trampled underfoot by the passers-by."[4]

Faced with this painful realization, Thérèse found great encouragement in one phrase. It was some words of St. John of the Cross: "One obtains from God all that one hopes for from him!"[5] God does not grant us his grace according to our qualities, virtues, or successes, but according to our hope. Here we have a liberating truth, which opens new doors! God lets himself be conquered by our loving hope. He cannot refuse his grace to someone who hopes for everything from him with childlike confidence! St. Thérèse realized that she should not hope for the holiness she so greatly desired on the basis of her own human possibilities, but only from God's grace, and she recognized that this grace would be given to her to the extent that she acknowledged her littleness and powerlessness and transformed both into a limitless hope in God's mercy.

> This desire [for holiness] could certainly appear daring if one were to consider how weak and imperfect I was, and how, after seven years in the religious life, I still am weak and imperfect. I always feel, however, the same bold confidence of becoming a great saint because I don't count on my merits since I have none,

but I trust in Him who is Virtue and Holiness. God alone, content with my weak efforts, will raise me to Himself and make me a saint, clothing me in His infinite merits.[6]

## HOPE AND POVERTY OF THE HEART

One of the essential dynamics of the spiritual life is the purification of hope. Hope has to be purified with regard to its object (our desires have to be oriented toward God, as explained above), but also with regard to its basis. What does our hope rest on? This purification sometimes needs to pass through the test of poverty.

At the beginning of our journey, we have, of course, a certain hope in God, but it is usually mixed with many other things: human ambitions and expectations, a degree of presumption with regard to our own capability, a search for human security to rely on, and a sort of unconscious bargaining—we try to merit God's blessings by our deeds. So God makes us pass through the sometimes painful trial of inner poverty. We experience how fragile and shifting all human realities are; we come up against our personal limitations; we are disappointed in some of our goals. If we consent to this path of impoverishment and stripping, we enter little by little into true hope: the hope that no longer relies on anything human, but only on God and his infinite mercy. We sometimes need to despair of ourselves or other people, in order to place our hope truly in God. As the Book of Lamentations says, "It is good that one should wait quietly for the salvation of the Lord. It is good for a man that he bear the yoke in his youth. Let him sit alone in silence when he has laid it on him; let him put his mouth in the dust—there may yet be hope" (Lamentations 3:26–29).

The fruit of this trial of poverty is the purification of our hope. We hope for everything from God, not because of any merit we might claim, or any human guarantee we might cling to, but only because God is God—because he cannot deny himself, he is faithful, and his mercy has no limits.

This is the act of boldness which we are sometimes called to make by the Holy Spirit: the more we experience our poverty and limitations, the more we set our hope on God alone! Holy Scripture says endlessly that whoever hopes in God will not be confounded: "I waited patiently for the Lord; he inclined to me and heard my cry" (Psalm 40:1).

Now more than ever, it is good for us to realize more clearly that true hope is the hope based on God's infinite mercy alone. It is the persevering, humble, loving practice of that hope which will obtain for us from God all that we need in order to follow our Christian vocation to the full.

---

**FOCUS:** Hope makes possible something that, humanly speaking, is impossible. It makes us confidently expect everything from God.

**REFLECT:** What is something impossible you can expect from God?

*Fr. Jacques Philippe, born in 1947, is a French priest belonging to the Community of the Beatitudes. With over one million copies sold in twenty-four languages, Fr. Philippe's writings on themes such as prayer, interior freedom, and peace of heart have become classics of modern Catholic spirituality.*

# A FATHER'S HOPE

## TOM PAGANO

*"Each of us is the result of a thought of God. Each of us is willed.*
*Each of us is loved. Each of us is necessary."*
— *Pope Emeritus Benedict XVI*

Two months ago, my beautiful wife, Megan, gave birth to our perfect little girl, Zelie Anne. Born 6 pounds, 11 ounces, and 22 inches long, every bit of her was precious. The moment I held Zelie in my arms, my life was forever changed. Sure, Zelie has certainly thrown our daily routines for a loop. My wife and I get less sleep than we used to and have fewer date nights out on the town. Preparing meals is trickier, and the laundry piles up pretty quickly. My golf game has suffered a bit, and I have less time to read and watch sports than I would prefer. Life has certainly been altered in these ways, but that was expected for the most part. However, a much deeper and more profound change has occurred—one that somewhat caught me off guard. When I became a father, it was as though a curtain was pulled back and my eyes were opened to an entirely new reality. In this reality I have found the reason for my hope.

Let me explain . . .

Simply put, there is no love like that of a parent for his or her child. If you have had the privilege of becoming a parent, then you know what I mean. This adorable, beautiful, pure, innocent baby is mine. Zelie trusts her mother and me entirely. She depends on us for her every need. When she is hungry we give her food. When she is tired we rock her to sleep. When she is cold we wrap her in her blankie. And what a joy it is to do this for her (even if it is three o'clock in the morning!). Zelie is completely vulnerable, and there is nothing I would not endure to protect her..

Recently Zelie and I have discovered our new favorite activity together. When we go over to Grandma and Grandpa's, we sneak away from the crowd and all the attention (Zelie sure gets a lot of attention at Grandma's) to sit on the front porch in their rocking chair. This is such sacred time for Zelie and me. We listen to the birds chirping, watch the animals scurrying around, wave at the neighbors walking by, feel the warm breeze, and, of course, rock. Sometimes we sit silently, sometimes we sing, and sometimes we pray. I spend time on the porch looking into Zelie's beautiful eyes, just thinking.

I think about the future. I wonder about the personality and temperament she will develop. I wonder what sports she will like to play, what instruments she will learn, where she will go to college, who she will marry. I dream about the first time she will see the beauty of a sunset on a warm summer night, or feel the peace of staring at the ocean while the waves crash on the shore, or the first time she experiences the triumph of climbing a mountain and gazing for miles over the landscape.

I also think about the state of the world she has been born into. What type of technological or medical advances will she live to see? Who will be the politicians leading our nation? In a time of unprecedented terrorism, countless mass shootings, and rising racial tensions, what type of world will Zelie experience? More than anything, I wish her success, health, happiness, and prosperity. However, the reality is that she may face hardships, failures, illness, and poverty.

This finally leads me to think about myself as Zelie's father. In these moments, I am confronted with the troubling reality that I will never be able to protect my beautiful baby girl from a world full of grief and violence and suffering. Not only will I not be able to protect her, but my love, despite my best efforts, will also fall short of what she deserves.

For some time I grappled with this combination of hope and fear for my daughter. It was within this context that I had a profound encounter with the reason for my hope.

It happened on the day Megan and I had Zelie baptized. Believe me when I tell you, much to my surprise, this day was more powerful and profound to me than the day Zelie was born! But that shouldn't be such a surprise. On that day I was reminded that Zelie isn't just the daughter of Tom Pagano. She is also the daughter of another Father, God the Father.

And what kind of Father is our God?

Our Father is King (Zechariah 9:9), Creator (Genesis 1:1), Savior (Psalm 3:8), Alpha and Omega (Revelation 1:8). Our Father is compassionate (Exodus 34:6), generous (Psalm 132:15), mighty (Zephaniah 3:17), wise and strong (1 Corinthians 1:25), and his kingdom has no end (Luke 1:33). Our Father is a Giver (1 Timothy 6:17), Helper (Hebrews 13:6), Healer (Psalm 30:2), and Miracle Worker (Psalm 77:14). And the best part is, this Father loves us in a way that is beyond what we can comprehend. He will let nothing, absolutely nothing, separate us from his love (Romans 8:37-39).

This truth overwhelmed me on Zelie's baptismal day. Zelie is a daughter of the King and an heir to the kingdom of God—a kingdom that extends far beyond this world. No matter what Zelie experiences in this life, she will always be the daughter of a King whose love for her endures forever (Psalm 126). If God is with her, who can be against her (Romans 8:31)? No sickness or disease, no hardship or trial, no failure or disappointment can separate her from the love of God the Father.

And this Good News is not just for my Zelie. We are all children of a loving God who wants to protect us and to provide for our every need. Ultimately, as much as I love Zelie, my love is just a drop compared to the Father's love for us. He loves each of us better than we can possibly imagine. And this is the reason for my hope.

This hope inspires my vision for the future: a vision not determined by the mess of the world but by the love of my Father. In this vision, I love Zelie to the best of my ability every day of my life. My imperfect love reflects the perfect love of God the Father, and Zelie allows His love to consume her heart entirely. She lives every day in the immeasurable peace, joy, and consolation that only the love of our Heavenly Father can bring. And finally one day, Zelie and I enter through the heavenly gates to dwell in the love of our true Father, together, for all eternity.

**FOCUS:** We are all children of a loving God who wants to protect us and to provide for our every need.

**REFLECT:** What dream inspires hope for your future ?

*Tom Pagano is a loving husband to Megan and an adoring father to Zelie Anne. The Paganos reside in northern New Jersey, where they enjoy the Lord's most abundant blessings through family, friends, and church.*

# THE PATH OF HOPE

## FR. J. MICHAEL SPAROUGH, SJ

*"Do not cast all hope away. Tomorrow is unthinkable.*
*Oft hope is born when all is forlorn."*
— *J.R.R. Tolkein*

I hope the Chicago Cubs win the World Series again this year. I hope the war in Syria soon comes to an end. I hope a more dynamic Catholic Church reaches more people. I hope to love Jesus and live with him forever. I hope we have Rocky Road ice cream for dessert.

Some hopes are more important that others, some dreams bigger than others. Proximate hopes are connected to our everyday desires and dreams. Ultimate hope is a theological virtue and is directly connected to the meaning of our life. Both are integral to dynamic living. Our spirit dies within us if we stop dreaming and hoping. But we must learn to hold proximate hopes lightly, while clinging with fierce determination to ultimate hope. Many proximate hopes get dashed along life's highway. While agonizingly painful, this can also be an extraordinary opportunity for growth.

I went to high school with the actor Bill Murray, star of *Ghostbusters*, *Groundhog Day*, and other popular films. In our sophomore year Bill's dream was to become a basketball star. He tried out for the team but got cut. He was crushed. Having nothing better to do, he decided to try out for the school play. Though cast in a relatively minor role, he drew laughter and admiration from the audience. A star was born!

Sometimes things turn around in unexpected ways for the better, but not always. Friends of mine adopted a young orphan girl from Ethiopia in the midst of that country's civil war and famine. They loved her, sent her to Catholic schools, and gave her every opportunity they could. But their daughter was so traumatized from the loss of her birth parents that she developed an attachment disorder, which makes it nearly impossible for her to trust anyone. Their hopes for her to live a happy life have not been realized.

In situations like this, we need to go deeper, to learn to live in ultimate hope. This is an active faith that God makes all things work to the good (see Romans 8:28). It's trusting that even deep suffering can draw us into God's love. Ultimate hope is accepting what is beyond our control and believing that God will use the circumstances of our lives to help us grow in holiness. When the words "Jesus, I trust in you" become more than a prayer, but instead a way of living, we are on our way to embracing the theological virtue of ultimate hope.

Bad things will continue to happen to good people. But ultimate hope clings to the belief that God is actively working in and through the circumstances of our lives so that we will come to know that peace of God that surpasses all understanding (see Philippians 4:7). Ultimately it really doesn't matter whether we're rich or poor, healthy or sick, good looking or ugly, smart or not-so-smart. What matters is that we discover the love that transforms us into people of hope. God's dream is for each of us to live in that great hope to which we are called (see Ephesians 1:18).

The saints are those who walk this path of hope. They choose to believe, in all the circumstances of their lives, that God is loving them into fuller life (see John 10:10). This hope is a choice, not a feeling. This hope is that God's divine love is leading us all through the unexpected twists and turns of life to a joy that is beyond our wildest, craziest imaginings (see 1 Corinthians 2:9).

I watched my best friend, Fr. Jim Willig, a diocesan priest from Cincinnati, pray for two years that the Lord would cure him of cancer. But the Lord did not answer his prayer in the way that Fr. Jim had hoped. Two years after his diagnosis, Fr. Jim died—despite having multiple surgeries and the most advanced medical treatments available at the time.

I watched Cardinal Joseph Bernardin of Chicago face the two greatest fears of his life: becoming a source of scandal for the Church he loved and dying of cancer like his father before him. Both fears were realized when Cardinal Bernardin was internationally disgraced by a false accusation of sexual abuse that I believe triggered the cancer that eventually took his life.

These two men of God both hoped and prayed for protection and health that were not given. On the surface their hopes were dashed. Cardinal Bernardin was disgraced, and both men eventually died of cancer. However, if we look deeper, another picture emerges.

Fr. Jim's cancer journey transformed him. In his book *Lessons from the School of Suffering*, he wrote, "The most helpful thing I have learned in my bitter suffering is to unite myself with Jesus on the cross, who unites himself with me on my cross."[7] Far from abandoning Fr. Jim in his time of trial, the Lord was transforming him into the man that he had always wanted to become. His prayer was fulfilled far beyond his greatest hope. He became, to many of us who knew him, a living saint who inspired a deep trust in God's love.

Cardinal Bernardin was eventually exonerated from the false accusation. He then took a profound step by meeting and fully reconciling with his accuser. Furthermore, they became friends, setting an example of hope for the world. Cancer took Cardinal Bernardin's life three years after the initial accusation. Yet, like Fr. Jim, Cardinal Bernardin was transformed, not defeated, by this journey. He wrote in his book *The Gift of Peace*, "[T]he good and the bad are always present in our human condition and . . . if we 'let go,' if we place ourselves totally in the hands of the Lord, the good will prevail."[8]

Fr. Jim and Cardinal Bernardin learned to trust that "suffering produces endurance, and endurance produces character, and character produces hope, and hope does not disappoint us, because God's love has been poured into our hearts through the Holy Spirit who has been given to us" (Romans 5:3–5).

Let's pray that we also are able to root our hope in God's power to transform us. We are "God's work of art" (see Ephesians 2:10). We are all saints in the making. Anything less than this will fall short of God's hope for us.

## AN ACT OF HOPE

When faith falters, virtue fails, and deeds of love are few,
Then, Lord, I pray that we may turn in hope to you.
So why are we disheartened when those whom we appoint
Reveal themselves as only human and inevitably disappoint?
May we hope not in our strength, wisdom, goodness, nor our
reason,
Not in our economy, technology, nor the latest, greatest of a
season.
Turn our eyes to you, Beloved One, beauty, ever ancient, ever
new,
Birthing hope, not of our own making but from you, in you,
through you.
Jesus, I trust your words of hope, cutting deeper than a knife:
"I've come in love for only this—that you may have New Life!"

---

*FOCUS:* What matters is that we discover the love that transforms us into people of hope.

*REFLECT:* In what situation is God calling you to become a person of hope?

*Fr. J. Michael Sparough, SJ, is a retreat master, storyteller, and writer at the Bellarmine Jesuit Retreat House outside Chicago. His weekly video blog can be heard at www.heartoheart.org.*

# PART TWO

# HOPE IN THE CHURCH

*"Such are the paths of all who forget God; the
hope of the godless man shall perish."*

—JOB 8:13

# THIS LITTLE LIGHT OF MINE

## JESSICA LUSHER GRAVAGNA

*"If we keep our eyes fixed on the Lord, then our hearts are filled with hope, our minds are washed in the light of truth, and we come to know the fullness of the Gospel with all its promise and life."*
— St. John Paul II

Fay and her husband sat down with their three kids to talk. Fay took a deep breath. This was going to be the worst moment of her life.

At thirty-nine Fay had been diagnosed with stage-four lung cancer. She didn't smoke. She had no family history of cancer. It was illogical and unfair, but Fay had a 15 percent chance of living past a year and a 5 percent chance of living two years. She looked at her thirteen-year-old daughter and tried to picture what it would be like to see her graduate high school. She imagined herself next to her husband, cheering her eleven-year-old on in football. And she wondered what it would be like for her five-year-old to receive his First Communion.

Fay had to do something no parent should ever have to do. She had to look into the eyes of her children and tell them she wasn't going to be with them as they grew up.

Fay may not have had control over when she died, but she could decide the kind of legacy she would leave. And in the midst of astounding suffering, Fay chose to leave a legacy of hope.

To find the strength to live and suffer well, Fay dove into the life of the Church. Many people in the small community Fay lived in watched in awe as they saw her at adoration, attending Mass, and living the life God gave her with peace and harmony, rooted in the power of love and prayer, despite her circumstances. Somehow in her weakness, Fay made everyone around her stronger. She even spent a lot of her time as a volunteer for hospice, comforting the dying.

When asked how she could live with such joy considering the circumstances, Fay would point to the Church. She would point to the place where she encountered a God who loved her enough to suffer, die, and rise again just for her. Fay would point to the reason for her hope: Jesus.

Miraculously, Fay lived for five years after her diagnosis. She saw her oldest graduate, she cheered her son on in football, and she witnessed her youngest receiving his First Holy Communion.

When she did pass, we learned that Fay had planned her own funeral. In classic Fay style, the funeral could best be described as a celebration. We all exited the funeral Mass singing "This Little Light of Mine" and clapping in joyous celebration. Can you imagine? There was not a heart unmoved in that church.

Fay's impact on my life goes beyond my ability to describe. Her beautiful witness to hope challenged me to be more than a lukewarm Catholic and inspired me to learn more about my faith. Fay will never cease to inspire me and lead me deeper into my faith and deeper into the Church.

But enough about me. Here are Fay's own words from her eulogy. As you read them, I pray that you will ask yourself the question: "If Fay can live with such hope, what is stopping me?"

———————

Greetings one last time to all my dear family and friends. You should have known who would have the last word! I want to thank all of you for coming here today to celebrate my life and to support my family and each other during this difficult time. It warms my heart just to think of all of you gathered together in my favorite place—the Catholic Church. I pray that you will truly see and appreciate the beauty of the church, the stained glass windows, the large crucifix, the statues, flowers, and candles. I hope that you really hear the glorious music and the spoken Word of God in the liturgy. May you smell the distinct smell of holiness that is seemingly present in all churches, and feel the renewal that comes through the holy water that is constantly flowing through the fountain. May you taste his promise to us in the bread and wine, his Body and Blood. I have spent many hours in this church—at Mass, in adoration, or just sitting alone in the presence of our Lord pouring my heart out and having it filled again. It has been these very things that have sustained and guided me during this most painful and difficult journey. The spiritual peace, strength, and even joy granted to me during my illness are impossible to explain except through faith. I know now, it is the only real reward worth seeking.

I know there will be times of pain, loneliness, and grief for those I leave behind. They are necessary components of true love. For proof of this, all you have to do is look up at the cross. But, beyond the pain is strength, beyond the loneliness is appreciation for life and others, beyond the grief is wisdom and hope—hope that we will all once again be united with God and each other in eternal glory forever.

John, Olivia, Luke, Sam, Mom, Dad, Troy, and Ben. When I look back on my life I am most thankful for the amazing family that I was blessed with. You are all incredible people and I hope and pray that you can go forward with joy in your heart, appreciating the time we had together and all the wonderful memories we created. Our time together may not have been the longest, but is was the best!

John, love of my life, my rock, my best friend, and my co-manager of the home. God doesn't make them any better than you. Don't worry. I will continue to pray for you daily. Olivia, Luke, and Sam. You were my pride, my joy, and my inspiration. As you leave the house every day, may you hear your mother's voice saying, "Make good choices!"

To my dear friends. You have been so important in my life. May you laugh often when you think of our time together (I know you will). I hope that the spirit of "Team Fay" will live on in your hearts forever.

As for me, I am the luckiest of all. I had a life filled with incredible family and friends, a career I loved, the best husband and children ever, fun, security, and most of all faith. What more could a girl ask for? Now I am planning to finally rest in eternal peace and glory with God the Father, the Son, and the Holy Spirit.

Until we meet again . . .
Fay

—*Fay's Eulogy, "Fay's Final Message"*

**FOCUS:** In the Church, we encounter a God who loves us enough to suffer, die, and rise again for us. We can point to the reason for our hope: Jesus.

**REFLECT:** If you were to write your own eulogy, what would it say?

*Jessica Lusher Gravagna is the cousin of Fay.*

# LIVE DIFFERENTLY

*CARDINAL DONALD WUERL*

*"One who has hope lives differently."*
*— Pope Benedict XVI*

Christ is our hope. Two successive popes, in visiting our country and particularly its capital, Washington, D.C., have proclaimed clearly this message. Over the portico of the Basilica of the National Shrine of the Immaculate Conception where Pope Francis canonized Saint Junípero Serra on September 23, 2015, these words are carved in stone: "Faith is the substance of things hoped for," or as the *New American Bible, Revised Edition* puts it, "Faith is the realization of what is hoped for." Pope Francis reminded us that it is precisely as people of hope that we continuously move forward. His predecessor, Pope Benedict XVI, in his homily at the huge Mass at Nationals Park on April 17, 2008, told us that those who have hope live differently.

What are some of the signs of our living out of the faith that gives rise to such constant and serene hope? When I look at the Church I am privileged to serve, I see countless manifestations of the substance or the realization of our hope.

Looking out from the altar or pulpit in the cathedral or many, many of our parish churches, what I see is the face of the world. Our faith community is made up of people from numerous ethnic and linguistic backgrounds, providing a rich mosaic of history and culture all united in one faith. Surely such communion is a witness to what Jesus spoke about when he prayed that we might all be one. Yes, there is still much more to do, but seeing so many faithful united in listening to the Word of God and celebration of the Eucharist with the commitment to go out and live that faith has to be a profound source of hope.

Yet the fount of hope flows in many, many life-giving streams. Throughout the history of the Archdiocese of Washington, Catholic laypeople, religious, and priests have generously supported the work of education, social service, and healthcare. All of these actions are manifestations of our Catholic identity, something that continues today even in an age of challenge. We recognize as Catholics that we do not make our way through life alone but as members of God's family, his Church. At that first Pentecost, the Spirit fell upon everyone, but gave different gifts to different people. To be a Catholic is to recognize the role of the Church as the very means created and given to us by Jesus so that work, accomplished in his death and resurrection, might be re-presented in our day and applied to us and those we seek to bring to Christ.

When we come to the institutions of the Church—its parishes, schools, universities, charitable organizations, healthcare facilities, and more—these all reflect a visible communion and at the same time are all founts of witness that are sources of our hope.

The Catholic identity of our schools is part of our hope for the future. Catholic education in all of its forms has as its primary task the communication of the person and message of Christ to adults, youth, and children. This unfolds through a wide range of efforts, but the goal is always the same. In our Catholic elementary and secondary schools, parish religious education programs, adult faith formation, the Rite of Christian Initiation of Adults, sacramental formation programs, and the many forms of youth ministry, campus ministry, and evangelizing outreach, the threads of the encounter with Christ and his life-giving message are woven into the fabric of our human experience. All of those engaged in this noble and life-giving effort are reasons for our hope for the Catholic Church as we move into the future.

But so, too, are all of our Catholic social service programs that have brought Christ's hope to those in need in our communities. Pope Francis tells us, "Our faith in Christ, who became poor, and was always close to the poor and the outcast, is the basis of our concern for the integral development of society's most neglected members." The many programs and outreach efforts of Catholic Charities, for example, are founts of hope. Guided by Catholic social and moral teaching and motivated by the Gospel message of Christ, Catholic Charities as we see it unfold in this archdiocese has extended a helping hand to the poor and vulnerable in a way that the face of God's mercy, love, compassion, and care is truly seen. And that same effort is found in the centers for children, teens, and families, in the affordable housing developments that, with Church involvement, provide shelter and related social services to so many low- and moderate-income senior citizens and families.

Another beautiful, inspiring, and encouraging fount of hope is found in the engagement of so many of our young people today in the mission and message of the Church. Our department of special needs ministries engages many young adults in supporting the spiritual development of our faithful with special needs and their families. But I also think of their involvement in our annual Rally for Life and in their participation in Catholic social services that touch so many people, giving them reason to hope. Here I would also add the compassionate care and healing that our Catholic healthcare entities provide and continue to make present in the lives of so many who look not only for healing but for hope. "The credibility of a healthcare system is not measured solely by efficiency, but above all by the attention and love given to the person whose life is always sacred and inviolable," Pope Francis reminded all of us.

The list of examples of where I find hope for the Church could go on and on. I cite these few simply to confirm what I say to the lay faithful, religious, and priests of this archdiocese with great regularity. Yes, there are challenges the Church faces, and yes, at times we might seem even overwhelmed by the secularism of our age, but we must look around us and see the faith, the strong love of our faithful in our parishes, the blessed hope they offer this and the next generation, and the expression of that same faith, hope, and love in all of the institutions, activities, programs, and ministries of this Church.

This may be an age of challenge, but it is truly a time of beautiful hope.

---

**FOCUS:** The fount of hope flows in many different life-giving streams.

**REFLECT:** How can your gifts and talents serve the Church in powerful ways?

*Cardinal Donald Wuerl is the Archbishop of Washington and the best-selling author of many books, including* The Catholic Way.

# IF IT ALL DEPENDS ON ME

## PATRICK McKEOWN

*"Our human compassion binds us the one to the other—not in pity or patronizingly, but as human beings who have learnt how to turn our common suffering into hope for the future."*
— *Nelson Mandela*

Life can change very quickly. Nine months ago I was a happy and healthy father of two. As I sit writing this, I am a happy father of three with a 50 percent chance of being alive in five years.

Nine months ago my wife became pregnant with our third child. Twenty-six weeks into the pregnancy, if it weren't for an incredible team of doctors and nurses and the grace of God, my son wouldn't be with us now.

It's been a difficult nine months to say the least, but it's also been full of hope. And if I've learned anything, it's that there is no hope if it all depends on me.

I want to share with you two moments in the last six months that have changed everything for me. They've changed my understanding of hope and opened the eyes of my heart to something truly remarkable.

Let's start with the birth of my son Max, my little man, my champ.

In my mind's eye I can still see the team of nurses and doctors as they rushed my wife out of the room. Max's heart rate was dropping, and if they didn't do an emergency C-section, he would die. I was left in the hospital room alone, unsure if my son was going to make it. And I was painfully aware of the reality that I could do nothing to help him or my bride.

In that hospital room I began to pray. I prayed for the doctors, for my wife, and for Max. I sent a text to Fr. Jacob, a dear friend and our pastor, as well as to the group of men from my Catholic Man Cave group. I asked them to pray for my wife and our son at their gathering that night.

I begged our Lord, our Lady, and St. Maximillian to safely bring our boy into the world. Almost immediately text messages lit up my phone. Sitting alone in that room, I was wrapped in a blanket of support and comfort. It was as if God were whispering, "Patrick, you're not alone."

Max was born that day weighing 2 pounds, 4.8 ounces. His frail, underdeveloped body was beautiful. I stood by helplessly as the team went to work, shoving tubes down his throat and into his skin. I couldn't believe how fragile he looked.

Fr. Jacob was right there beside me, and he baptized my son. Come what may, death no longer had a hold on Maximillian.

Relief swept over me as I looked around at the group of people that had saved my son's life. It wasn't until later that night that things began to sink in. I began to feel those familiar nerves and surges of joy that all dads share after their children are born. I spent that night with the nurses, enjoying pizza and wine while my wife, Keegan, slept. During that evening, a thought began to emerge: Thank God none of it depended on me!

The ninety-seven days that followed in the NICU were full of constant reminders that I was not in control. I could give my son nothing other than my time and prayers. At the end of that time, I had the incredible joy of carrying medicine, tubes, and oxygen to the car as we brought Max home—swaddled and delicate—to his brother, Paddy, and sister, Marie.

Then came my diagnosis.

Just one week after bringing Max home, I had a growth removed from my head. The doctor reported that it was melanoma—a deadly form of cancer that pegged me with a fifty-fifty shot at living more than five years. The surgeries, chemotherapy, fatigue, and nausea that followed stretched our already-challenged family. For a while all I could do was lie in bed, clutching a blanket my prayer group knitted for me, simply trying to survive each day.

As a husband, a father of three, and a Catholic school teacher involved in his parish, I was used to protecting, supporting, providing, and serving those around me. But it was becoming clearer and clearer that I had to live in a new reality—a reality I didn't much like.

I couldn't remove the cancer that was eating away at my body. I couldn't feed my kids. I couldn't make a dent in our growing medical bills. I couldn't even mow the lawn. I couldn't do anything!

Between my son's premature birth and treatment and my diagnosis and treatment, things began to really look bleak financially.

I remember talking to my mother-in-law, wondering how in the world we were going to stay afloat. She decided to set up a GoFundMe page with descriptions and pictures of our situation. As humbling as it was, we needed the money. Keegan and I thought, *Why not?* We expected maybe four thousand dollars to be raised.

Within two weeks over six hundred people gave a total of fifty-four thousand dollars.

Take that in with me for a second. In fourteen days six hundred people—some total strangers—raised fifty-four thousand dollars on our behalf.

Keegan and I sat in the kitchen laughing, as the total continued to rise, because what else can you do when something extraordinary like that happens? Families from the parish, people I'd known in high school but hadn't interacted with in years, strangers, friends of friends all gave generously of what they had.

At one point, someone stopped by our house with an envelope. This guy was on his way to take his eighteen-month-old daughter to have her fourth major surgery.

"Who was that?" Keegan asked.

I replied, wide-eyed, "I think it was a friend of a friend." I held up the envelope. "It's a thousand dollars." Like Han Solo encased in carbonite, we were in stun mode. Who were these people and why were they helping us?

And it wasn't just monetary help either. People rallied around us to do all the things I could not. They delivered meals, mowed the lawn, and watched the kids. They sent text messages and flowers and let us know they were praying for us.

The generosity of God's family infused our lives with hope. They helped me look in the eyes of my children and tell them everything was going to be okay. And I could do that precisely because none of it depended on me!

With the help of Simon of Cyrene, Jesus carried his cross to Calvary. In my time of need, six hundred Simons responded to God's call to help our family carry our cross.

A lot of individuals think, "What can I do?" But perhaps it's time to start thinking, "What can my parish family do?" I've gone to church my whole life, and it never occurred to me to wonder how much my parish could accomplish if we helped pick up the crosses of those in need right in front of us.

God's Church stood up for me and my family in a huge way. Whether it was the prayers of my men's group, Fr. Jacob being there to baptize Max, the six hundred who gave generously of their money, or the countless people who helped us get through daily life, we were witness to something incredible. And you know what is even more incredible? There is nothing particularly special about my family or my parish. The stunning truth is, what happened to me can happen in every parish in America. There isn't anything that can stand in the way of God if his people respond generously to his call to love one another as he loved us.

Take a moment and imagine what your parish could do for those in need if every parishioner gave what they could. Everyone can do something, and it all makes a difference. Even delivering a meal or mowing the lawn can change everything for a family in need.

If everyone gave what they could, the Catholic Church would be the brightest light the world has ever seen. My hope is that my parish and yours don't wait a second longer to become everything God has dreamed they could be.

There is no hope if it all depends on me. There is no hope if it all depends on you. But if we work together . . . well, now that's a different story, isn't it?

**FOCUS:** Nothing can stand in the way of God if we respond generously to his call to love one another as he loved us.

**REFLECT:** How can your parish respond to God's call to help carry someone else's cross?

*Pat McKeown is the proud husband of Keegan and father of Paddy, Marie, and Maximilian—as well as babies Ignatius and Jude, whom he and Keegan didn't have the joy of knowing in this life but look forward to knowing in the next.*

# ANSWERING THE CALL

## FR. JONATHAN MEYER

*"It is Jesus who stirs in you the desire to do something great with your lives, the will to follow an ideal, the refusal to allow yourselves to be grounded down by mediocrity, the courage to commit yourselves humbly and patiently to improving yourselves and society, making the world more human and fraternal."*
— *St. John Paul II*

This is a story about a young man, a God who loves him, and a Church that provided hope in a moment of great need. I feel blessed to have been a part of these events, and I pray it encourages you along your journey.

The story begins at 9:30 at night. I was still in my office when the phone rang. I picked it up and said, "St. Luke's, this is Fr. Meyer." There was a little bit of silence, and then I heard his voice.

"This is Will."

"Will, it's 9:30. What's going on?"

We chatted for just a few minutes and made plans to meet the next day.

I had met Will that morning at his Catholic high school's Lenten reconciliation service. At the end of three hours hearing confessions, the crowd of students finally began to thin. I started to leave, but I saw a young man begin to walk toward me. It was Will.

He tried to go to confession but couldn't. Instead, he just sat in front of me sobbing. At the end of what seemed like an eternity of him crying, he got up to leave. I wasn't sure how to help him, so I said, "You need to talk to somebody. I don't know what you're going through, but people can help you. I don't know what church you belong to, but if you want to call me, I'm at St. Luke's." He thanked me and left.

I didn't expect him to call, but he did. So I met with Will every day for two weeks straight after that. During our first meetings, Will would do nothing but come into my office and cry. Slowly but surely, though, Will began to open up about the immense pressure and anxiety he felt in his life. This talented, driven, smart young man was completely overwhelmed and at his breaking point.

To relieve some of the pressure in his life, I encouraged Will to become a part of our community life at the parish.

In short order, Will joined our youth group and became an altar boy. He started coming to Mass every single Sunday. He found a great group of young men, whom he could call brothers. Within the parish, Will was filled with hope—hope that his life had meaning and value beyond the grades he got or the college he got into. Will found a place where he could be loved simply because he was as a child of God. All of this . . . changed Will's life.

But I didn't know the extent of the impact until five years later.

I had become pastor at a different parish, which had a school. Attending the school was a young boy in the seventh grade named John. John lived a difficult life. His parents were divorced. He lived with his dad in our small town. His mom, who struggled with drugs and addiction, lived in the big city. He often bounced back and forth from homes, but his dad was his bedrock. He loved his dad.

One day, John's dad tragically died. I remember, after the funeral, sitting at a table with John's mother, a lot of members of the family, and a lawyer. The decision was made that our school was going to keep John and provide him with a home, a place to stay, and food to eat. It was tough, but we all knew it was the best decision for John.

As a parish we gave John food, a place to live, and a great education. But no matter how hard we tried, John, understandably, battled despair. It was physically palpable. I could see it in how he carried himself, how he engaged with his classwork, and in his interactions with others. I became deeply worried for John's life.

In a moment inspired by the Holy Spirit I was reminded that I knew someone who might be able to speak into John's circumstance with greater depth and meaning than I could. So I called Will up and said, "Will, you have no idea who this kid is, you'll probably never meet him, but he's struggling. And he just needs a good man to tell him that it can be OK—to have hope and to believe that it's going to be OK." Will agreed.

A few days later in the mail, I received a handwritten letter from Will to John. When I opened the envelope, there was a Post-It on the outside of the letter that said, "Father, please read this first." The letter went something like this:

Dear John,

My name is Will. When I was a senior in high school, I felt that my world was falling apart. I decided one day to take my life. I sat down with a priest in a gym, and I tried to tell him what I was going to do, but I couldn't get the words out. All I could do was cry.

That afternoon, I made the decision that I was going to follow through with my plans. And yet, in one last effort, I made a deal with God that, if this priest answered the phone, then I wouldn't do it. So I called this priest at 9:30 in the evening, and he answered his phone.

From that point on, I gave my life to Christ, and through prayer, through good friends, through the Church, my life is changed. I've now graduated from college, I'm engaged, and life is good.

Writing this, even now, some ten years later, I get emotional. I never knew how close Will was to suicide. He almost gave in to despair, but in his darkest hour, Will allowed God to fill his life with hope. His letter was his attempt to do the same for John.

I took the letter and gave it to John. The impact was significant. But still John needed something more.

A few weeks later after the letter I received a save-the-date for Will's wedding. Again, inspired by the Holy Spirit, I took the save-the-date card for Will's wedding, pulled John out of class, and gave him the card, saying, "John, Will just told me that he wants you to serve his wedding."

That never happened. I lied. But I knew that Will would want John to serve his wedding, and I knew that John needed something to live for and something to look forward to. Knowing he was going to meet Will gave John hope.

On the day of Will's wedding (I was the presider), I remember opening the door to the church for John. Will was already inside waiting for him with open arms. He gave John the biggest bear hug I've ever seen. Will then put his arm around John, walked him directly into the Church, and sat him down in the back pew. I have no idea what they talked about, but I will tell you this: After that, John was changed. He had hope. He began to believe that his future could be bigger than his past, that God loved him and would give him everything he needed to get through the trials of life, and that heaven was on his side.

So where are you on your journey? Are you like Will when I first met him? Are you battling despair and in need of hope? If so, I implore you, be like Will and give God a chance! Go to your parish family and to the sacraments. Don't be afraid to let God love you wherever you are at.

If you are resonating more with where Will was when he met John, thank God! But don't be complacent. Be like Will and become someone who is waiting with open arms to give hope to those who need it, no matter the cost. Be a part of a parish who goes above and beyond to care for someone in need, even the needs of a stranger. After all, you never know when a life might depend on it.

---

*FOCUS:* When we allow God to transform us, we can be agents of change for others.

**REFLECT:** Who in your life could benefit from a letter of encouragement? Now what's stopping you from writing that letter?

*Fr. Jonathan Meyer is a priest and pastor from the Archdiocese of Indianapolis who loves his ministry. He spent his first five years as the archdiocesan director of youth ministry and has spent the last eight years bringing parish communities together in different arrangements, mergers, and closures.*

# PART THREE

# HOPE IN ACTION

*"Through him we have obtained access to this grace in which we stand, and we rejoice in our hope of sharing the glory of God. More than that, we rejoice in our sufferings, knowing that suffering produces endurance, and endurance produces character, and character produces hope, and hope does not disappoint us, because God's love has been poured into our hearts through the Holy Spirit who has been given to us."*

—ROMANS 5:2-5

# A GOD OF MIRACLES

## LINDA MALIANI

*"For a Christian the situation is never hopeless. A Christian is a man of hope. That is what sets us apart."*
— *St. John Paul II*

Bath time in our household had become a routine. After three children, my husband and I were seasoned professionals at knowing what to expect when we got each child into the tub. February 12 was the same as any other evening—until I noticed something unusual. I had taken our youngest, two-year-old Alyssa, out of the bathtub to dry off when I saw a big lump on her neck.

My husband and I knew that couldn't be normal, but we had no idea how bad it was. The doctors found a mass in her abdomen the size of a grapefruit. Because the tumor was wrapped around all her major blood vessels, they told us it was inoperable. Alyssa had stage-four neuroblastoma.

This was a burden too big for such tiny shoulders. After all, tiny Alyssa only weighed twenty-five pounds.

From that day on, doctor after doctor told us there was no hope for a cure for Alyssa. They mostly said things like, "We are going to give Alyssa the best we have, but even our best cannot cure her." Others said, "We can treat this, but, at best, we can only give you a couple of years with her." Doctors told us that Alyssa had no hope of living—and that we had no hope at all.

I remember her falling asleep in my arms one night. I laid her on the floor, knelt next to her, and prayed, "God, I don't know where you are, but I have to find you." God whispered back in the quiet of my heart: "I am in the Church."

Now, I surely was not where I should have been or where I wanted to be in my faith, but I knew it was God talking to me. So I figured I'd better listen.

I began going to Mass every day. Many Sundays going to Mass had been difficult or impossible with three children, but suddenly daily Mass became the most hopeful part of each day.

As I heard stories about Jesus in the readings at Mass, I marveled at how far people would travel just to touch him, to be in his presence, and to be healed by him. They hoped against all hope that Jesus was the miracle worker they had heard so much about.

Like the people in the Gospels, I was in need of a miracle. So every day I went to Mass and prayed and hoped Jesus would heal my baby girl.

We asked our family and friends to pray for a miracle for Alyssa. Although there seemed to be no hope in the eyes of the doctors, we believed we could find hope in a God of miracles. And we wanted everyone to carry this hope and this prayer with us.

During the months of rigorous therapy, one of my cousins had a friend who drove St. Teresa of Calcutta from place to place when she was in New York, and my family had the opportunity and great honor to attend Mass with Mother Teresa. After we received Holy Communion, Alyssa started to cry. My husband and I walked out into the hallway with Alyssa, trying to calm her down. Mother Teresa followed us out, carrying three Miraculous Medals in her hand. She put one on Alyssa and told us to wear the other two. Then Mother Teresa taught us a simple prayer: "Mary, Mother of Jesus, make our baby all right." She prayed this prayer with us over and over again as we stood in the back of the church. At the time, it was very difficult for me to pray this prayer, but she urged us to pray it over and over again with her.

Up to this point, Mother Teresa was very serious as she prayed. But suddenly a huge smile broke out over her face. As if God had spoken to her while she was with us, she completely relaxed and then said, "She's going to be fine, and she's going to grow up!" As she began walking away from us, she turned around, smiled, and said again, "She's going to be fine, and she's going to grow up!" And with those incredible words of hope, she left. We clung to those words and began to pray as she taught us.

After many months of chemotherapy, on the day of Alyssa's second surgery my family once again gathered at the hospital. During her first surgery, the doctors had removed 75 percent of Alyssa's tumor. Now the doctors wanted to go back in for a second surgery to try to peel the remaining tumor off her aorta and other blood vessels. We were prepared for another seven-hour surgery and continued to pray for a miracle.

Thirty minutes into the surgery, the clinician came to us with tears in her eyes and told us that when they opened up

Alyssa, there was no visible tumor, dead or alive, to remove. Apparently Alyssa's insides looked as though she had never had a tumor at all. There was not even any scar tissue from her first surgery. They had never seen this happen before. One of the doctors told us that if she had not been in the room for the first surgery, she would have thought they had operated on the wrong baby.

My husband and I, after months and months of praying with our whole hearts for a miracle, were in shock. It was like a scene straight out of the Gospels. God had healed Alyssa, and we, the witnesses, were amazed.

As I sit writing this, twenty-seven years later, I enjoy watching my beautiful Alyssa bathe her own two babies: my granddaughter and grandson. Her oldest, Maria Teresa (named after St. Teresa of Calcutta), recently turned two, the same age Alyssa was when she was diagnosed. Alyssa's family has its own bath time routine now, and I am privileged to watch.

I don't pretend to understand miracles or how and why God does some of the things that he does, but I do clearly know who healed my daughter: God. Now that is where I place my hope.

---

**FOCUS:** In the end, the most important miracle of all is heaven. Therefore, in life and in death, whether we see our miracle or not, we can always have hope.

**REFLECT:** What miracle do you need God to do in your life? Use this space to write out your request. It will be more real for you when you can see it in writing.

*Linda Maliani has been married to Pete Maliani for thirty-nine years, and they have four children and nine grandchildren. She currently teaches religion to sixth, seventh, and eighth graders.*

# SOUL SEARCHING

DEREK GAZAL

*"Hope allows us to enter into the darkness of an*
*uncertain future to journey in the light."*
— *Pope Francis*

Something was missing in my life.

On the surface everything seemed to be going well. I was living out my dream as an artist. My band was playing with groups like the Black Eyed Peas and the Roots, with artists like Kanye West, Jimmy Cliff, Robert Randolph, and so on.

But success came at a high price.

I was twenty-five thousand dollars in debt and had every reason to believe that if I kept going along this path, that number would continue to rise. Worse yet, I had this unshakable restlessness that often left me feeling miserable. Clearly something was out of whack in my life.

In the midst of my search for answers, I had a heart-to-heart conversation with the drummer of my band. We discussed everything from religion to relationships to politics. It was in that conversation that he challenged me to tithe. Even though I grew up Catholic and considered myself a pretty faithful guy, I had never heard of tithing. He explained to me that tithing is giving "10 percent" of your money to God.

My reaction was, I think, very reasonable, given my circumstances. "What? No way, man. You're crazy!" I knew I was no financial expert, but I was pretty sure the solution for someone in debt was not to give 10 percent of his income away.

Nonetheless, I felt challenged by my friend. My perception of myself at the time was that I was already a good Catholic, and he presented a concept that made me question that. I honestly was not aware of the spiritual bankruptcy that was deeply affecting my life. So when this man, whom I deeply respected and trusted, challenged me to go deeper, it caused me to stop and consider it.

Challenged, wanting more out of life, and not really sure what to do about this "tithing" thing, I started praying and doing some research.

Eventually I found my way to the Book of Malachi. As a prophet, Malachi encouraged the people of his time to tithe:

> Bring the full tithes into the storehouse, that there may be food in my house; and thereby put me to the test, says the Lord of hosts, if I will not open the windows of heaven for you and pour down for you an overflowing blessing. (Malachi 3:10)

Giving away 10 percent of my hard-earned money didn't seem like the way to go for me, but "opening the floodgates of heaven"—that one seemed like a good fit for my life! I wanted those blessings. I NEEDED those blessings, so after much spiritual resistance and negotiation with the Holy Spirit, I took a leap of faith and started tithing.

In order to appropriately tithe, for the first time in my life, I made a budget that included all of my income. That budget opened my eyes to how detrimental living beyond my means was. I know that seems obvious, but until I had the numbers in front of me, I didn't know how immense—but also how simple—my problem was. Once on paper, the debt no longer seemed insurmountable. The way forward looked difficult . . . but doable. God was opening my eyes and showing me the way out of debt.

A budget, of all things, filled me with hope. It filled me with confidence that God really did have an intimate knowledge of my heart, that he truly knows what's best for me.

God took this act of faith and gave me the courage to grow more disciplined. And not just disciplined with how I spent my money, but also in how I spent my time. Like Jesus says, we cannot serve two masters. So I left my band, moved back in with my parents, stuck to my budget, and gave my day job the attention it deserved. Most people in my life, including my drummer, thought I was a bit off the charts for making these types of radical changes. But the results spoke for themselves, and praise God, I paid that debt off in two years.

Most importantly, during that time, my soul exploded with life, and my faith grew exponentially. Quiet time with the Lord, prayer, reflection, Mass, adoration, confession, and almsgiving became my lifeline. My faith was on fire!

Tithing seems really risky at first, especially in the midst of debt. But, man, was it good for my soul! It stretched me beyond what I thought I was capable of and brought my life to a place I never could have dreamed was possible. It taught me that God does really pour out blessing without measure.

Tithing was a turning point in my life and I am eternally grateful for it. Through it, God changed my heart. He helped me to become, not just a man who talked about trust, but a man who lived it. I didn't know it at the time, but God wasn't doing this just because he wanted me out of debt or just because he wanted me to work harder at my job. He did it because he was preparing me for my true calling in life. He was preparing me to meet my wife.

Not long after I started tithing, literally a week or two, I met my future wife in the most unlikely of places. Ten thousand miles of land and ocean separated us, and what everyone including my mother thought was impossible became possible. We now have two beautiful, healthy little girls, are business owners, have founded a charity, and share our faith together in home, parish, and community. Instead of restlessness and frustration, my life is filled with peace, joy, and hope. A hope that knows God does amazing things when I trust in him.

By placing God first in my financial life, it opened up every other aspect of my life and opened up the floodgates of heaven for me!

Of course, tithing isn't the only means God uses to guide us along life's journey. There are many personal as well as communal things one can do to grow in faith. For example, the Catholic Church is filled with jewels of wisdom, hope, and ultimately love for the journeying believer. While it seems almost counterintuitive at first, the decision to step out in faith, take a risk, and bet on the wisdom of God is a decision that turned my life upside down in the best way possible. It brought my heart from death to life.

Through my experience, I've learned that hope is a gift from God, and it is a gift I desperately need. God promises us that doing his will on earth, without exception, will be worth it, and whether we receive his blessing on this side of heaven or the other, we must believe this to be true.

Life can be hard. It can be difficult to navigate, but with hope in Christ as my light, surely no darkness can ever overcome me. I pray that my heart and yours will remain open to God and his bride, the Church. May this hope bring us peace in the present and hope for a better tomorrow.

---

**FOCUS:** The decision to step out in faith, take a risk, and bet on the wisdom of God is a decision that never ceases to fill the soul with deep peace and true hope.

**REFLECT:** What's standing between you and an intimate, hope-filled relationship with God?

*Derek Gazal is the founder of St. Joseph's Outreach, a charity whose mission is to build faith in the community through the power of prayer and create or strengthen a relationship with local parishes. He is also known as the pop-rock-reggae artist Blindman and volunteers for witness talks at parishes through McKenna Stewardship when possible.*

# NADIA

## REBECCA RECZNIK

*"Hope begins in the dark, the stubborn hope that if you just show up and try to do the right thing, the dawn will come. You wait and watch and work: You don't give up."*
— Anne Lamott

The youngest of my two sons had just turned a year old when I began to feel the first flutters of new life again in my belly: another human being. I was not expecting or planning to be pregnant again. Many women dream of the day they find out they will be new mothers. But no one ever tells you what to do if that day comes and you feel apprehensive instead of excited.

I tried to shake my anxiety. But even after I had my morning cup of coffee and my two toddler boys had finished smearing oatmeal on their pajamas, even after they were tucked safely into their beds for the night and the dinner dishes were done, the darkness lingered. It nipped persistently at my soul.

I would look at experienced mothers around me with vans full of kids and wonder how they did it. I was aware of the profound responsibility of raising little ones, and it filled me with dread. I read stories of strong, steadfast mothers in the Bible, and they haunted me. How could a mother find such strength? It seemed impossible and, quite frankly, insane.

When my first two sons were born, I suddenly became more aware of sin and suffering in the world. The violence made me nauseous, much worse than morning sickness. I felt overwhelmed by the amount of evil that existed.

How could I bring another little life into such a troubled and chaotic world?

I felt hopeless and alone in a dark, angry world. I could not imagine seeing my children in a world where I couldn't protect them. That terrified me. I could not see hope.

Then one day, my husband insisted that I start practicing gratitude amidst the anxiety. Seeing how anxious I was on a daily basis, he said, "God is not coming to you through this fear." He was right: My anxiety surrounding motherhood dimmed my awareness of God's love in the world. This was no way to take on the challenges of parenthood. This was no way to overcome fear. This was no way to find hope.

My husband encouraged me to name one thing—just one thing—every day for which I was grateful. Together we entered into this practice of thanksgiving in our daily lives. When I prayed, I would grapple for one thing to be thankful for every day. The experience of finding gratitude was really tough; I could see only an empty cup. For the first few weeks, I really felt that I had no reason to thank God.

It took a while, but eventually I started to name one thing each day that I was grateful for. Many days I thanked God for my sons and for the child growing inside me. As the days and weeks continue to unfold, I discovered that, no matter how difficult or burdensome the day was, there was always one thing in particular for which I could be grateful: motherhood itself.

A warmth was returning to my soul.

Around that time, we began to pick out names for our sweet unborn baby, trying to narrow it down to several options since we had not found out the gender. We had a lot of trouble sifting through all the boy names that we liked, but, ironically, we could agree on just one girl name.

A close priest friend of ours once told us that naming a child was a serious business and should not be taken lightly. Ever since we've approached naming our children with deep prayer and attention to detail, knowing that our child would stand before the Lord with that name.

My husband wanted to incorporate some of his strong Polish heritage into the baby's name. He wanted our child to feel the deep roots of tradition, community, and family life that grew beneath him or her. No matter what kind of world our baby was born into, he or she would not be alone.

I continued to fight feelings of anxiousness until my precious baby girl was placed into my arms. As I felt her little body against mine, I cried and cried, gratitude flooding my soul again. This was hope. She was hope. This was the face of sweet, precious hope incarnate. In that moment, hope became not just a word, but a living being to me.

We named her Nadia, which is Polish for "hope." Her middle name, Jane—a tribute to my late grandmother—means "God is gracious."

Hope became a living being to me as well as a daily experience. Each morning as I hear the birds singing outside of my window and I smell the coffee brewing, it's not long before I reach down toward my little girl in her crib and she reaches back up to me. As I pick her up and draw her close to my heart, I realize again that hope is not a feeling, but an action. A decision. My husband and I made the choice to hope with the conception of each child, and it is a commitment to God that I renew every morning as I take my children's chubby hands in mine and guide them through each day.

Nadia Jane is my uncalculated, unplanned, and un-questioned YES to God. And by looking at this life and my little family through the lens of the eternal, I find my hope. One life can change so much. Who knows what my little Nadia will do, how she will bring God's love into the world? With each new life, with each YES, we give Christ a chance to enter the world and let the light of God shine amidst the darkness.

---

**FOCUS:** One life can change so much. With each YES, we give Christ a chance to enter the world and let the light of God shine amidst the darkness.

**REFLECT:** What is God giving you the chance to say YES to today?

*Rebecca Recznik happily stays at home and explores the world through the eyes of her four mud-loving, chalk-drawing children on their ten acres of country in Michigan. In her few moments of spare time, she enjoys dabbling in photography, reading a good book, and sleeping.*

# AN ANNIVERSARY TO REMEMBER

## MARGUERITE BRAMBANI

*"Love is a mutual self-giving which ends in self-recovery."*
*— Fulton J. Sheen*

Austin and I have celebrated forty wedding anniversaries. My favorite anniversary, by far, was our twenty-ninth; it was one of the best days of my life. It was on that day that I had my most profound encounter with hope.

In my mind hope and purpose are directly tied to one another. Without an understanding of purpose, there can be no hope. Take a knife, for example. Knives were invented for the purpose of cutting things. If you try and use a knife to start your car or unlock your door, it's hopeless! You will not open your door and you will certainly not start your car. In fact, you will probably do more damage than good.

Knowing the purpose of something and using it for that purpose brings hope. It's true for little things like a knife, and it is true for big things like a marriage. Without knowing the purpose of marriage, how can a relationship thrive? Spoiler alert: It can't!

Let me explain using my own marriage as an example.

For the first half of our marriage, Austin and I treated raising our twins as the purpose of our marriage. I fully immersed myself into their daily lives, doing my best to teach them the Catholic faith and make sure their days were filled with joy and love. Austin focused all his energy on providing a good living for the children and me. He worked endless hours and made sure we had everything we needed.

Raising children and raising them well is a noble endeavor and we did our best, but I was haunted by the fear of what would happen to our marriage when our children were grown and out on their own. Would there be anything left to salvage?

We lived such separate lives. He worked, and I raised our children. It was a lonely life and a lonely marriage. There wasn't much fighting or arguing. There wasn't much communication at all. I wanted us to have a better relationship, and he did too, but we just didn't know how to get on the same page. We didn't know how to make our marriage work.

Austin's parents divorced after twenty-five years of marriage, and a part of me was resigned to the idea that the same fate awaited us. Talk about being hopeless!

As I said, no purpose—no hope.

Then one afternoon God intervened in my life. I often visit a local Catholic bookstore for inspiration and guidance. On this particular day God inspired me to pick up an audio CD. Something about the title, *Becoming the Best Version of Yourself*, caught my attention. I thought, *Well, I certainly don't want to be the worst version of myself!*

As I listened to the CD in my car, everything changed. Like being hit by a bolt of lightning, I came face-to-face with my purpose—and more importantly, my neglect of that purpose. God created me to become a saint, or as the CD put it, God made me to become the-best-version-of-myself.

Rather quickly I began to feel things changing within me. I was filled with an energy fueled by purpose, and I had an overwhelming sense that things could get better. For so long I had played the role of the victim, but it suddenly occurred to me that I didn't have to. After years of feeling helpless, I suddenly felt hope swell within me.

I had been so busy trying to change my husband, fix my marriage, and raise my children that I stopped trying to become the-best-version-of-Marguerite. I stopped getting better. But if I could vow at that moment to dedicate my life to my God-given purpose, then I knew there would be hope for me—and hope for my marriage.

Now, this hope was not the hope you hear in popular conversation. It was not synonymous with wishful thinking. Instead it was synonymous with possibility! Holiness was possible, fulfilling my God-given purpose was possible, and having a positive impact on my marriage was possible!

I was so excited that I couldn't wait to ask Austin to listen to the CD with me. We went on a long car ride, and he listened to the whole thing straight through. The CD struck him in the same way that it had struck me. That day in the car was the start of what has become a daily conversation. We ask each other, "What can I do to help you become the-best-version-of-yourself today?"

We started to become a team. And day by day, little by little, our marriage improved. We became committed to helping each other become the-best-versions-of-ourselves. As a result our marriage has become infused with purpose and driven by the hope that we can help each other get to heaven.

Our twenty-ninth wedding anniversary is my favorite because on that day my husband came into the Catholic Church. It was the day he fully committed to the purpose of our marriage and welcomed the Church into our marriage as the source of wisdom and grace we need to live life well. It was the day we welcomed hope into our lives and into our marriage.

And what a beautiful day it was!

---

*FOCUS:* Without an understanding of purpose, there can be no hope.

*REFLECT:* How will becoming a better-version-of-yourself impact the relationships around you?

*Marguerite Brambani is a devoted wife, mother, and grandmother who loves God and her family above all else. She lives each day with gratitude in her heart for all her blessings and offers her daily prayers for a more peaceful world.*

# ORDINARY GRACE

## *TALIA WESTERBY*

*"What gives me the most hope every day is God's grace, knowing
that his grace is going to give me the strength for whatever I face."*
— *Rick Warren*

If you were to spend a week observing my life, it would seem
completely normal, boring even.

Every day I get up roughly at the same time, I do the same
tasks, I eat the same set of meals, I see the same people, I go
to Mass in the same place, and I watch the same TV shows.
Of course, having young kids, my routine can get turned
sideways, but to be honest most days look kind of the same.

I consider this normalcy to be a miracle.

Mental illness nearly robbed me of any hope at leading
a normal life. But God, through everyday, ordinary people,
rallied to save me.

This is my story, and I am honored to share it with you.

———

Something wasn't right. I knew that much. I wasn't exactly sure what was going on, but I couldn't move. I felt weak and confused. My mind was cloudy. I could hardly think.

I was left with one clear thought—call Dad!

Ring, ring.

"Dad. I am not bleeding or physically injured, but something is terribly wrong with me."

After sitting through several doctor's appointments and tests, I learned that I had had a severe panic attack, brought on by increased stress in my life; a car accident, a challenging teaching position in the inner city, a broken engagement, and my mother's second diagnosis of breast cancer had all contributed. It became clear that I needed to seek intense treatment for obsessive compulsive disorder and bipolar disorder.

My parents whisked me away from Indiana to move in with them in Wisconsin, so I could receive specialized care at a nearby clinic. I felt both blessed to live with my parents during this time and incredibly isolated from my friends and routine.

At this point, my life could have gone one of two ways: the way of despair or the way of recovery. There were two key turning points in my journey to recovery.

The first came in the form of a decision.

Shortly after I was diagnosed, I spent several hours each day in therapy or working on exposures back at home, slowly rebuilding my life and learning how to live with OCD and bipolar disorder. Sometimes I met with a group of others like me, other times with a psychologist, and also with a psychiatrist. While it was helping, the doctors suggested I take medication in addition to my therapy.

I wasn't sure if I wanted to. Being a woman of faith, I felt like I should have been able to pray my way out of it, like my illness was the result of a lack of faith on my part.

But the thing was, the psychologist and psychiatrist were helping. God was working through humanity and the remedies of the world. Just like the accounts in the Gospels, God was meeting me where I was.

As I spoke more with the doctors, they explained to me how mental illnesses are due to a chemical imbalance. So, the more I thought about it, the more I began to believe that if God could work through humanity, he could also work through medication.

I chose to start taking medicine in addition to my therapy in order to allow myself the stability to be the person I knew God intended me to be.

The results were amazing! I was able to hear and follow the Lord's plan for my life in an entirely new way. What a relief! Who knew that God could answer prayers through professional help and medicine? I found—and continue to find—hope in a God who lives and works through people in my everyday life.

My second turning point came when I started attending my sister's Catholic young adult group on a weekly basis.

I was reluctant to go at first, but when I did, I encountered something incredible. These people were awesome! They attended Mass together, went to confession regularly, and held each other accountable to living good, moral lives. At the same time, they could still go out and a have a pint together! Who knew something like this was possible?

Most importantly, they did not question what had me briefly in Wisconsin. Instead, they simply accepted me and loved me. When I was around them, I didn't feel different, I felt loved. I can't tell you what a gift this is to someone suffering with a mental illness.

Doing life with incredible people who inspired me to be the person God created me to be provided me with a support system and filled me with hope. Hope that I could lead a normal life again, that I could be loved again, and that this storm would pass.

―――――

Through the grace of God and the help of many, many people, I have weathered the storm. Although I like to joke that I am "cured," I will always notice when picture frames are crooked and need to keep things in order. My friends will jokingly ask me to come over to help clean and organize their homes and desks, because I enjoy doing that kind of thing—and do it quite well!

I will always have plenty of charming quirks. My life will include an ongoing struggle with mental illness, and that will come with plenty of challenges and trials, but I rest assured that the Lord will offer me hope in my brokenness, through professional help, prayers, community, and in ways only he knows.

Today, I strive to be a source of hope for those carrying the cross of mental illness. I want people to hear my story, to learn that I suffered a really difficult experience, to see where I am now, and to have hope that they can experience healing too.

I also want to challenge the Church to become better a better version of itself. Rarely do I hear petitions for those suffering from mental illness. We often shy away from talking about the signs, struggles, and decisions surrounding a mental illness diagnosis. There are so many people struggling in our communities who feel cut off from the love of God. For the Church of Christ, this has to be unacceptable.

I am really fortunate to have found a strong community in Milwaukee. We need more strong Church communities to help carry us along the way. There is no organization, institution, or ministry in a better position to serve those with mental illnesses than the Catholic Church. I am living proof of that. But we need to step it up a little bit.

So, where do I find hope? I find hope in good doctors who work hard to relieve the suffering of their patients, who spend countless hours serving a seemingly endless stream of suffering. My hope is in the Catholic Church, an incredible community full of good, faithful, loving people who do God's work through ordinary, everyday acts of love.

My hope is ultimately in a God who refused to put down his cross on the way to Calvary but who didn't refuse a little help from a stranger along the way.

---

*FOCUS:* We can rest assured that, even in the most trying times, God will answer our prayers—just not always in the way we might expect.

*REFLECT:* What are some of the ways God has answered prayers in your life?

*Talia Westerby is the executive director of Arise Missions in Milwaukee, Wisconsin, and has the blessing of spending much of her time with her husband, Carl, and two sons, Maximilian and Theodore, who keep her on the road to holiness!*

## PART FOUR

# BECOMING

# HOPE

*"[B]ut they who wait for the Lord shall renew
their strength, they shall mount up with wings
like eagles, they shall run and not be weary,
they shall walk and not faint."*

—*ISAIAH 40:31*

# SCHOOL OF HOPE

## ARCHBISHOP JOSÉ H. GOMEZ

*"I plead with you—never, ever give up on hope, never doubt, never tire, and never become discouraged. Be not afraid."*
— *St. John Paul II*

The story of Cardinal Francis X. Nguyen Van Thuan is one of the most harrowing and inspiring of the twentieth century.

Cardinal Thuan had just been named coadjutor of the Archdiocese of Saigon when the Vietnamese communists seized power in 1975 and imposed a brutal dictatorship. They threw Archbishop Thuan in prison, where he suffered for the next thirteen years—nine of which he spent in solitary confinement.

During these years he prayed and wrote messages to his people on scraps of paper that were smuggled out and later published.

The constant theme of his writings was hope.

The ability to pray—to talk to God—gave him a sense of freedom, even though his body was in chains. In that dark night of solitude, with no human contact, he found hope in God. And as a result, he has become for our times one of the Church's great witnesses of Christian hope.

"Christians," he said, "are the light in the darkness, the salt where life has no savor, and [the] hope in the midst of a humanity which has lost hope."

Cardinal Thuan died in 2002 and is being considered for sainthood. I reflect on him these days, as I think about the continuing persecution of Christians in the Middle East, Africa, and elsewhere in the world. I pray every day—as I believe all of us in the Church should—that those suffering persecution may persevere in hope.

Hope is the theological virtue that enables us to keep our eyes on heaven—even during those times when our sufferings and trials make our lives here on earth seem like a living hell.

By the gift of hope, infused in us at baptism, God helps us to trust in the good news of Christ Jesus, and to await confidently the blessings he has promised to those who believe in him.

Christian hope is not some kind of wishful thinking—far from it! Christian hope is the only certainty in this passing world. Pope Benedict XVI said this very powerfully in his 2007 encyclical letter on hope, *Spe Salvi*.

All the "hopes" of this world are contingent and temporary. People hope for many things: work, material comforts, love, and happiness. But these things, no matter how essential and beautiful, don't necessarily last. We can lose our job, we can lose a loved one, and we can have our freedom or our good health taken from us. If we have no greater hopes than these, we are bound for a life of disappointments and sadness.

Christian hope, the hope of the cross, is not like that. St. Peter said: "By his great mercy we have been born anew to a living hope through the resurrection of Jesus Christ from the dead" (1 Peter 1:3).

So what are we hoping for? We hope for the fulfillment of Christ's promise—that we who believe in him will have eternal life (see John 6:47, 54).

What we hope for as Christians has already come true. Christ has died, Christ is risen, and Christ will come again. What we expect in the future—heaven and eternal life, salvation and redemption—has already been guaranteed.

Because Christ has been raised from the dead, we can be certain that he will raise us, too, to eternal life. When we live with this kind of hope, we are free even if we are in chains, as Cardinal Thuan was.

Our hope in the Resurrection should animate every aspect of our lives. But like all the virtues, hope is hard to hold onto.

Despair is the opposite of hope. We can look at all the sadness and suffering in the world, perhaps even in our own lives, and be tempted to despair. It is, in fact, one of the great temptations we face when we look at the world today.

We see plenty of signs that things in the world are not the way God wants them to be. We see war and poverty, persecutions and terror. We see all the injustices and inequalities, including the routine taking of innocent human life through abortion, that are going on in our society. Sometimes, it can seem like we are a long way from the kingdom we are called to build as Christians.

We know that millions of our neighbors feel abandoned, as if God has forgotten them. They observe all the chaos, all the evil and injustice, and they can't imagine that a "good"

God could allow this. Some have grown bitter and reject God. Others have grown indifferent and live as though God does not exist.

This is a real challenge for the Church's mission of the new evangelization—and I think this is a special task for Christians at this time in our history: We need to teach the world how to hope again! As Cardinal Thuan said, Christians are called to be a light in the darkness, in a world in which so many have lost hope.

We need to help our brothers and sisters to rediscover the beautiful plan of God for creation, his Providence and love. God is in charge. We know that by faith. He is in charge of history, and he is in charge of our individual lives. And that means that we matter to God—each one of us.

This is what Christian hope teaches. And this beautiful message must be one of the key themes of our new evangelization.

Pope Francis calls hope the virtue that is hidden and humble. Hidden—because so often we do not see reasons for our hope in the world. Humble—because our hope is made real in the humility of Jesus, who comes to walk with us, to share our life, our joys, and our struggles. He says:

> This virtue of hope . . . is so hard to live. [It is] the smallest but strongest of the virtues. And our hope has a face: the face of the Risen Lord. . . . The triumph of Jesus at the end of time will be the triumph of the cross, the demonstration that the sacrifice of oneself for love of neighbor, in imitation of Christ, is the only victorious power, the only stable point in the midst of the upheavals and tragedies of the world.[9]

So we need to help our brothers and sisters to persevere in hope, even amid the struggles and challenges of our daily lives. We need to bring them to the encounter with the Risen Jesus, who is the cause of our hope. In order to do that, first we need to grow in this virtue ourselves. We need to have a positive plan to nurture the growth of this virtue in our lives.

Prayer is the great school for growing in hope. When we pray we realize that we are never alone. This is the hope that kept Cardinal Thuan going during those long years of isolation. And he has good advice for us: "There is no need to be formal, simply pray from the heart—as a child to its Father."

My prayer is that all of us will set aside time daily for these simple conversations. We should make time to pray for our loved ones and ourselves. But we also need to pray that the star of Christian hope may rise in the hearts of all our brothers and sisters. And let us make a conscious effort, in all our actions, to be a source of hope for others—through our words of encouragement and our works of love and mercy.

As Cardinal Thuan said: "The road of hope is paved with small acts of hope along life's way. A life of hope is born of every minute of hope in that lifetime."[10]

Let us pray for that gift of hope and let us ask our Blessed Mother Mary, Our Lady of Hope, to help us to always stay close to Jesus, following him with love, and being missionaries of his hope.

---

**FOCUS:** We need to have a positive plan to nurture the virtue of hope in our lives. Prayer is the great school for growing in hope.

**REFLECT:** Think of someone you would like to pray for. And then pray this prayer: God of the Resurrection, give _____ a heart of hope.

*Archbishop José H. Gomez serves as the archbishop of Los Angeles and as the vice president of the United States Conference of Catholic Bishops.*

# INSTRUMENTS OF *GIALLO*

*MSGR. GENO SYLVA, STD*

*"The secret of everything is to let oneself be carried by God
and so to carry Him to others."*
— *St. John XXIII*

Location, location, location! How blessed I am to have such a glorious vista! I believe that my office window at the Pontifical Council for the Promotion of the New Evangelization provides me with the finest view in the Eternal City. No, I do not gaze upon the architectural splendor of St. Peter's Basilica or catch verdant glimpses of the manicured Vatican Gardens. Rather, my vista encompasses the walkway that, during the Jubilee Year of Mercy, was reserved for the Jubilee pilgrims. It began at Castel Sant'Angelo, followed its way down the Via della Concilizione, continued through the Holy Door of the Basilica, and ended fittingly at the tomb of the apostle Peter. Each day I witnessed thousands of pilgrims from every corner of the world making this sojourn, praying and singing in preparation for their deepening conversion into Christ as they passed through the Holy Door during the Jubilee Year of Mercy.

These wayfarers came dressed in every color in anticipation of a once-in-a-lifetime opportunity to receive the special graces made available to us during that year by Pope Francis. Yet, as I looked down upon the throngs of people, one color stood out above all the rest. Scores of men and women were dressed in bright yellow Jubilee vests and hats as they guided the pilgrims along this roughly five hundred yards of joyful expectation. These were the Jubilee volunteers who made it possible for each pilgrim to have an undisturbed spiritual experience despite the scorching Roman sun, the pelting rain, or the often rude and intrusive tourists. Each Saturday a new group of thirty to one hundred Jubilee volunteers arrived to begin this selfless service of mercy. There were over three thousand people ranging in age from eighteen to eighty-five and from thirty-six countries who hearkened to this call. They included retired men and women, college students, seminarians, priests, housewives, religious sisters, deacons, military personnel, and unemployed young adults.

Why the color yellow? When we first met to discuss the uniforms which would make the volunteers easily distinguishable to all, I vehemently objected to the suggestion that they be yellow. Growing up in the United States, I can vividly remember some children using the phrase, "What are you, yellow-bellied?" to indicate a person who is cowardly or easily scared. Thus, for me, yellow has always had a negative connotation. On the contrary, my Italian colleagues assured me that in their country yellow (*giallo*) has always been associated with clarity, sunshine, and, yes, even mystery. In fact, a twentieth-century

Italian literary genre is specifically known as *giallo*, taking its name from the trademark yellow covers of these little books. Introduced in 1929, they were works of mystery and suspense that captivated the Italian people during the harsh times of deprivation in which they were living.

As I continued to observe the volunteers, I saw how truly *giallo* each one had been. They displayed a certain clarity of purpose. They did not want their names to be remembered, but they did want to provide more than mere access to the Holy Door of St. Peter's. By their very presence, attentiveness, and bright smiles, they demonstrated to each pilgrim that his or her life did, indeed, have great value. Many pilgrims commented to me that they were overwhelmed by the care given to them by those strangers dressed in yellow. One elderly man said he went through the Holy Door three more times because he felt much more worthy of God's love after having been treated in such a caring and kindly manner. How reflective of the pastoral approach of Pope Francis! As Archbishop Rino Fisichella, president of the Pontifical Council for the Promotion of the New Evangelization, described the Holy Father's emphasis upon personal encounter, "It is love that generates faith, and faith which sustains love. . . . Someone believes that he or she is loved." I often saw how overwhelmed the pilgrims became when they encountered these volunteers who unknowingly provided further reasons to believe simply by the witness of their loving examples.

But even with the clear facts that these people traveled to Rome for a most noble purpose and were easily recognizable by their golden garb, there was still a sense of mystery about them. Why were they performing such unselfish deeds? How could they leave their jobs and their families to assist at the Jubilee of Mercy? Both pilgrims and tourists alike asked me numerous times about what the Vatican is paying them. They were incredulous when I replied, "Only with box lunches and rooms for the night." Their sacrifices reaffirmed in my own mind that these individuals were true instruments of the mystery of our Christian faith—a dazzling light which exceeds our understanding, rather than something unknown and hidden. As Pope Francis told a group gathered in St. Peter's Square on October 15, 2013, "Christian hope encompasses the whole person, so it is not a mere desire or an optimism, but the full realization of the mystery of divine love, in which we have been born and in which we already live."

According to the Holy Father, hope is not a feeling or an emotion but a conviction that comes from knowing that we are loved by God. And in some small way, each of these volunteers dressed in *giallo* is not a fictional character in an old Italian suspense novel but a witness to the true mystery of divine love. Since the deprivations of today are often spiritual, these volunteers fortified each pilgrim as he or she crossed the threshold of the Holy Door and served as personal examples of the hope that comes from Jesus Christ. I feel very fortunate that I was able to catch glimpses of these "instruments of *giallo*."

---

**FOCUS:** By your very presence, attentiveness, and bright smiles, you can demonstrate to people around you that their lives have great value.

**REFLECT:** How can you become an "instrument of *giallo*" in your life? Could you encourage a friend or a loved one in some way? Could you write a thank-you note to someone who might not be feel appreciated? Could you provide a meal for someone in need?

*Msgr. Geno Sylva, STD, is a priest of the Diocese of Paterson serving on the Pontifical Council for the Promotion of the New Evangelization.*

# THE ABC'S OF HOPE

## *ALLEN R. HUNT*

*"We rejoice in our hope of sharing the glory of God."*
*— Romans 5:2b*

Babies inspire hope. My wife and I learned that today. Our first grandchild just arrived in the world. A new generation appearing right before our very eyes. Little Allen Joseph. His birth has opened a dimension of my heart I did not even know existed. He has introduced me to love in a whole new way. So I write to him now of my hope for his life and for his faith.

Dear Allen Joseph,

Your grandmother and I have deep hopes for you. These are my ABC's of hope for you.

**A** good priest – Is there anything better for a boy, a teen, and a man to have in his life? May your life be filled with many fine priests.

**B**aptism – My eyes will fill with tears when my daughter holds you to receive the waters of baptism. What a gift! New life in the family of God. All the possibilities. May you not only know who you are but also whose you are.

**C**aring teachers – The greatest gift we can give you is the gift of faith. I pray for caring teachers throughout your life to show you the way and to help you embrace it.

**D**eep love for people – Jesus teaches us to do two things: 1) Love God. 2) Love people. I am not concerned with whether you attain wealth or recognition. May you be known most of all for your deep, deep love.

**E**aster people – After all, that is who we are. One man said, "If you don't believe in the resurrection, then you're not a believer." We are Easter people. I hope you will learn to look forward with desire and confidence. With that, you will have a hope that the world does not.

**F**unerals – May you be inspired by funerals, because we are Easter people.

**G**reat education – I hope you have a fine mind. Even more so, I hope for an education that truly prepares you for life. To think fully. To have the "mind of Christ."

**H**eart for God – I pray you will be like King David. A man after God's own heart.

**I**nspiring music – May your ear be filled with the melody of God. Whether it be "In Christ Alone," or "Be Thou My Vision," or a tune I have not yet heard.

**J**esus on the crucifix – When I sit and listen to my friend as he musters every ounce of courage to endure chemo treatments, he and I look at the crucifix, to our suffering Lord. I pray, my grandson, that you experience that same hope in your own times of confusion, pain, or despair.

**K**nowing where you are headed - Our citizenship is in heaven. An old Jewish Hebrew name for God is The Place. I want you to know that's where we are going. You are destined to be in Him. God is our Place.

**L**ove - It has always defined the Church and God's people. Love sets us apart from the world. We love. That will make you different.

**M**onastery of the Holy Spirit - I spend a retreat day there each month. The sheer beauty of the architecture in the church alone lifts my heart. I hope to share that same inspiration with you very soon.

**N**ot alone - You are not alone. Ever. We are surrounded by a great cloud of witnesses, people of mission who lived life well. We shall meet them face to face when we too reach The Place.

**O**utstanding sense of vocation and purpose - Whether called to be a priest, or to single or married life, I pray for you to embrace a life filled with divine purpose. May that purpose animate your world every day.

**P**arents - When I see parents sitting with their children at Mass, praying with their kids in a restaurant, or serving on a mission team as a family, I sense the deepest hope imaginable. Those parents get it—they are investing in their kids' souls. And that will make all the difference. May God bless your parents as they seek to do the same for you.

**Q**uests - Think St. John Fisher. Willing to lose everything, even his life, in his quest to love God and to be obedient. Quests will remind you, my little boy, that you can be better and better. And you will be.

**R**eception into the Church - Who can be at the Easter Vigil Mass and witness a young man affirming his faithful desire to become a part of the Easter People and not feel hope? I look forward to the day you fully enter the Church.

**S**aint Gertrude the Great – What a woman! I hope you get to know her a bit in your life. The only female saint to be called "the Great." It's easy to see why. Read her prayer and it becomes obvious. She is a lady of great hope.

> O Sacred Heart of Jesus, fountain of eternal life, your Heart is a glowing furnace of Love. You are my refuge and my sanctuary. O my adorable and loving Savior, consume my heart with the burning fire with which yours is aflame. Pour down on my soul those graces which flow from your love. Let my heart be united with yours.

**T**he Eucharist – The Body. The Blood. The Eucharist changed my life and my soul. I hope it will feed and nourish you every day of your life.

**U**nconditional love – For just a moment, meeting you, my grandson, drew me into the heart of God, a heart filled with unconditional love. If I, as a flawed earthly grandfather can love you like that, I can only begin to imagine how much God's unconditional love abounds for you.

**V**ery generous people – people who give are the hope-iest people I know. May you become one of them.

**W**ork ethic – Everyone in your family seems to have a great one. I hope you get one too.

**X** – The first letter for Christ in the original Greek. X was a symbol for Christ in the early Church. The dictionary says a "hope" is a person in whom expectations are centered. For you, my grandson, I pray that person will be Jesus. After all, he is the Christ.

**Y**ou remind me I am not alone – I will help you discover that we are on this journey of hope together with many good people.

**Z**ephyr – A fresh wind—there is one blowing in the Church—can you feel it? May it inspire your life today, tomorrow, and forever. Amen.

Love,
Your Hope-full Grandpa

---

*FOCUS:* We are Easter people, looking forward with confidence. With that, we have a hope that the world does not.

*REFLECT:* Create your own ABC's of hope for your life or that of someone you love.

*Dr. Allen R. Hunt is a speaker and bestselling author at the Dynamic Catholic Institute.*

# HANDS OF HOPE

## GRANDPA HESS

*"Christ has no body now but yours."*
*— St. Teresa of Avila*

I have the hands of a Midwestern farm boy. They are weathered and coarse. They are sun-dried and calloused. They are tired and bruised. My hands have tilled soil and planted seeds. They look every bit of the ninety-three years of life I have lived.

I have the hands of a husband. They have fixed cars and changed lightbulbs. They have stained the fence and changed the oil. They have mown the lawn and taken out the garbage. My hands are uniquely formed to hold the hand of my bride of seventy years. They never feel quite as good as when they are in hers.

I have the hands of a father, grandfather, and great-grandfather. They have changed diapers of forty-five of the most beautiful children, grandchildren, and great grandchildren a man could ask for. They have dried tears, played catch, wrapped presents, rocked cribs, tickled toes, and fed each child with love.

I have the hands of a son. They shook my father's hand as I left for World War II, and they held my mother tight when I returned home. They have gripped the shovel as I buried both of my earthly parents. My hands have opened the good book written by my Heavenly Father. They have held the Body of Jesus Christ every day for over seventy years.

Ultimately my hope rests not in the work of my own hands, but in the hands of Jesus. Jesus has been with me every day of my life. I felt this most powerfully the day I kissed the wounds of Christ on the hands of the great saint Padre Pio.

I met Padre Pio during my third year serving as a bomb site auto pilot mechanic in World War II. When the war ended, I was asked to remain in Europe for an extra year of service. My family contacted me from home in Ohio and told me they thought I was stationed near San Giovanni Rotondo, where Padre Pio lived. Sure enough, when I looked at my map, I realized I was in the town right next to San Giovanni Rotondo. Can you believe that? What are the chances? It had to have been the Lord!

The first time I met Padre Pio, he allowed a group of us to kiss the glove covering the stigmata on his palm. What a grace! I was deeply moved by his presence. There was something different about Padre Pio. His presence was weightier than others'. He was always joyful, always smiling, despite his painful wounds. It was a gift for him to suffer with the Lord. I felt closer to God when I was with Padre Pio, and I couldn't wait to visit him again.

God gave me the opportunity to visit Padre Pio on four occasions during my time in Italy. I remember him inviting a fellow soldier and me to kneel before the altar as he said Mass. We were so close to him that we could clearly see the stigmata on his palms as he celebrated the Eucharist. He always took off his gloves for Mass. We received the Body of Christ from those hands. Later, he invited me to kneel in front of him, placing his right hand on my head and holding his left hand out in front of me. I kissed the wound of Christ in Padre Pio's flesh. That experience was such a special grace. I think about it every day.

The only time I spoke to Padre Pio was to ask him to pray for my sister and father, who were both in poor health. My mother had written me from home to request this prayer intention from him. After hearing my request, he said to me, "I will keep them in the palm of my hand." I knew they would be taken care of. And they were.

I can feel Padre Pio with me all the time. I know he is praying for me and my family. On the day Padre Pio died, the bells at our church tolled miraculously for almost three hours. The janitor had to clip the wire near the bells to make them stop. I could hear the bells tolling out on the farm nearly a mile away. That was Padre Pio's way of saying good-bye to us. Sometimes when I close my eyes, I can still hear those bells ringing and I smile.

The saints are beacons of hope in the world. They show us that ordinary men and women can be the living hands of Jesus acting in the world. Saints show the world that God does powerful things through those that make themselves available to him.

Padre Pio gives me hope that one life can make a difference in another. He gives me hope that my hands can do God's work. Even through a simple Midwestern farmer, husband, father, and son, God can bring hope into the world. If God can make a saint out of an ordinary man like Padre Pio, he can do the same thing with you and me.

In my life, hope has been found in people. It is through people that God has shown me how he loves to do the extraordinary through the ordinary. My wife is my hope. My children, grandchildren, and great-grandchildren are my hope. Padre Pio is my hope. Jesus is my hope. You are my hope.

Yes, you reading this, you are my hope. You are a gift from God to the world. You hold within you the hope of a greater and more beautiful Church. You hold within you the hope that this can become a nation of holy families and saintly priests and religious. You hold within you the hope that love can prevail over hate. You hold within you the hope that God will bring the wonderful message of salvation to every corner of the earth.

You are the hands of God in the world. Go now and make him something beautiful.

---

**FOCUS:** Hope is found in people. Through people, God shows us how he loves to do the extraordinary through the ordinary.

**REFLECT:** Name the people in your life that bring you hope. Reach out to one of those people this week, and thank them for being a source of hope for you.

*Grandpa (Paul) Hess is a retired farmer and veteran of World War II. He has seven children and has been married to his wife, Mary, for seventy years.*

# ENDNOTES

1. http://www.dictionary.com/browse/hope?s=t.

2. http://www.dictionary.com/browse/wish?s=t.

3. *Dialogue of St. Catherine of Siena: The Treatise of Prayer.*

4. John Clark, OCD, *Story of a Soul: The Autobiography of St. Thérèse of Lisieux*, Third Edition (Washington, DC: ICS Publications, 1996), p. 207.

5. *Dark Night of the Soul*, Book 2, Chapter 2.

6. John Clark, OCD, *Story of a Soul: The Autobiography of St. Thérèse of Lisieux*, Third Edition (Washington, DC: ICS Publications, 1996), p. 72.

7. Rev. Jim Willig with Tammy Bundy, *Lessons from the School of Suffering* (Cincinnati: St. Anthony Messenger Press, 2001), p. 22.

8. Joseph Cardinal Bernardin, *The Gift of Peace* (Chicago: Loyola Press, 1997).

9. Angelus (November 15, 2015).

10. Francis X. Nguyen Van Thuan, *The Road to Hope* (New York: New City Press, 2013).

# NOTES

# NOTES

# NOTES

# NOTES

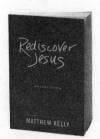

# Blessed

## THE DYNAMIC CATHOLIC FIRST COMMUNION & FIRST RECONCILIATION EXPERIENCE

There's never been anything like this for children: World-class animation. Workbooks with 250 hand-painted works of art. Catechist-friendly leader guides, and incredible content. Blessed isn't just different, it's groundbreaking.

Request your **FREE** First Communion Program Pack & First Reconciliation Program Pack at *DynamicCatholic.com/BlessedPack.*

### EACH PROGRAM PACK INCLUDES:

- 1 DVD SET (42 ANIMATED SHORT FILMS)
- 1 STUDENT WORKBOOK
- 1 LEADER GUIDE
- 1 CHILDREN'S PRAYER PROCESS CARD

*Just pay shipping.*

**Dynamic Catholic**
Be Bold. Be Catholic.®

# HAVE YOU EVER WONDERED HOW THE CATHOLIC FAITH COULD HELP YOU LIVE BETTER?

How it could help you find more *joy* at work, *manage* your personal finances, *improve* your marriage, or make you a *better* parent?

## THERE IS GENIUS IN CATHOLICISM.

When *Catholicism* is lived as it is intended to be, it elevates every part of our lives. It may sound simple, but they say *genius is taking something complex and making it simple.*

*Dynamic Catholic* started with a dream: to help ordinary people discover the *genius of Catholicism.*

*Wherever you are in your journey,* we want to meet you there and walk with you, *step by step,* helping you to discover God and become *the-best-version-of-yourself.*

To find more helpful resources, visit us online at DynamicCatholic.com.

 **Dynamic Catholic**

*FEED YOUR SOUL.*